CONTENTS

C000137330

FOREWORD BY BARRY HINDSON

"Football's Coming Home" is a phrase that has come into the language more out of hope than expectation, but if you amend it to the "The Vase is Coming Home" it takes on a whole new level based on reality.

The relationship between North East football and the FA Vase has become unique and I was privileged to witness the almost seasonal triumphs of the last decade and a half through my coverage of the finals on BBC Newcastle.

Like the rest of the local football population I have wallowed in the success.

There are so many highlights to consider, from the initial triumph of Newcastle Blue Star in 1978 when Ian Crumplin scored the winner in the last minute against Barton Rovers,

Imagine that.

A West End lad scoring the winner at Wembley in the last minute of a national cup final to bring the trophy to the North East.

Then Colin Richardson magnificently cajoling and bullying his Whickham side to victory.

These, though, were relatively isolated successes.

It was not until Villa Park in 2002 when Ian Chandler's headed extra time winner had me dancing around the BBC studio like a whirling dervish that the party really began for me.

Even then, I had to wait until the end of the decade before Whitley Bay's extraordinary hat-trick of victories really sealed the magical bond with the Vase and laid the foundation of glories to come.

It has never been the same since.

An all-Northern League final between Dunston and West Auckland in 2011 gave Michael Dixon the opportunity to emulate his father who had been a winner with Blue Star.

The following season the gentlemen of Spennymoor proved too much for the ragged lads of Tunbridge Wells.

Sholing denied West Auckland a second tilt before normal service was restored with North Shields' extra-time winner against Glossop.

Morpeth overcame the bookies' odds and 20,000 opposition fans to thrash

NORTHERN GOAL

Hereford and the following season South Shields were comfortable winners over Cleethorpes.

That was my last Vase Final for the BBC but it will not be my last trip to the twin towers, or arch, as it is these days.

Like thousands of others I regard the Vase as part of my football heritage.

It has been a fabulous personal experience for me to enjoy so many Vase triumphs over the years.

To have the opportunity to re-live those experiences through "Northern Goal" is marvellous.

Mark writes with the kind of personal and passionate prose only someone who understands what the Vase means to us can produce.

It is a book written with authority, insight, wisdom and humour, and I recommend it without reservation. If you love local football you will love "Northern Goal."

Barry Hindson

Barry Hindson is a North East non-league football expert with over three decades of experience behind him.

He spent just under thirty years working for BBC Newcastle reporting on non-league games around the region and was also the co-author of 'We Just Love Football' and 'We Still Love Football'.

Barry now provides expert opinion on the North East Football Podcast and is still heavily involved in the non-league scene.

Image: Peter Talbot (South Shields FC)

CHARITIES

Motor neurone disease (MND) is a fatal rapidly progressing disease that affects the brain and spinal cord, attacking the nerves that control movement so muscles no longer work.

It kills a third of people within a year and more than half within two years of diagnosis.

It's a devastating disease that affects up to 5,000 adults in the UK at any one time and kills six people every day. There is no cure.

The MND Association is the only national charity in England, Wales and Northern Ireland focused on MND care, research and campaigning.

Denise Davies, Head of Community Fundraising at the MND Association, said: "Without the amazing support of people like Mark, the MND Association simply would not be able to provide its vital support services, fund research to find a cure and campaign and raise awareness of MND. Together we are making a real difference for people affected by this devastating disease."

For more information on the Motor Neurone Disease Association go to https://www.mndassociation.org/ or follow them on Twitter @mndassoc

This book has been produced in support of the Motor Neurone Disease (MND) Association. The MND Association is the only national charity in England, Wales and Northern Ireland focused on improving care and support, funding vital research and campaigning to raise awareness for people affected by MND. The charity relies on voluntary donations. 50 percent of the profits raised through the sale of this book will be donated to the Association. Find out how you can get involved at www.mndassociation.org

Registered Charity number: 294354

NORTHERN GOAL

Suicide is the silent killer that devastates lives across the world, every 40 seconds someone, somewhere, takes their own life. In 2017 there were 6,213 recorded deaths by suicide in the UK and Republic of Ireland.

If U Care Share Foundation was founded in 2005 after Daniel O'Hare took his own life at the age of 19. Daniel was in the prime of his life with a family that loved him, great friends and a good future ahead of him.

His family to this day still does not know why Daniel chose to take his own life.

Since then his family set out trying to keep Daniel's memory alive by sharing a lifesaving message – "There is always a way"

IUCSF has three main aims: Prevention, Intervention & Supporting those bereaved by suicide.

They have delivered workshops to almost 26,000 young people in schools, colleges, universities and professional football clubs.

In addition, IUCSF have also now supported over 1500 individuals who have been devastated by suicide.

"OUR AIM IS TO PREVENT ANYONE FEELING THE PAIN WE FELT AS A FAMILY WHEN WE LOST DANIEL. WE TRULY BELIEVE THAT TALKING CAN SAVE LIVES."

Shirley Smith, Co-founder of If U Care Share Foundation

For more information on the If U Care Share Foundation go to https://www.ifucareshare.co.uk/ or follow them on Twitter @ifucareshare

This book has been produced in support of the If U Care Share Foundation The charity relies on voluntary donations. 50 percent of the profits raised through the sale of this book will be donated to the Foundation. Find out how you can get involved at www.ifucareshare.co.uk

Reg. Charity Number 1142001

INTRODUCTION

There is something special about football in the North East.

It ignites something deep inside the soul of people from a largely working-class region.

Passion for the game flows through their veins like the Rivers Tyne, Wear and Tees flow through the region's major towns and cities.

It gives hardworking folk a reason to battle through the monotonous grind of everyday life, knowing that Saturday brings a release of the senses.

The pre-match chat, the slow walk to the ground, that feeling of taking your place inside the stadium, at the same spot you have stood or sat year-after-year.

The post-match recriminations, debates about players, goals, decisions, followed by the Sunday morning analysis of the papers, simply putting off preparing for a return to the Monday morning grind.

But supporters of the region's three "big" clubs have been left wanting when it comes to genuine success.

They show pride and commitment in abundance but they are rarely rewarded by seeing their heroes lifting silverware on the biggest stages that the game can offer.

Newcastle United, Sunderland and Middlesbrough have all won second-tier titles in recent years but they have won only three major trophies between them since the 1960s.

Only Boro's Carling Cup win in 2004 has been achieved since we somehow avoided the impending doom that was the Millennium Bug.

There is success in the region's game but you have to go well beyond the emerald green turf and bright lights of St James Park, the Stadium of Light or the Riverside Stadium.

Success can be found a world away from the millionaires plying their trade in front of tens of thousands of supporters paying well over the odds, surrounded by cameras provided by multi-billionaire backed broadcasting companies.

True success has been achieved by school teachers, plumbers, long-distance lorry drivers, office workers and postmen.

They have put the daily grind behind them to make their names, not as ordinary working-class folk, but as footballers, representing the region's non-league clubs with honour and pride.

NORTHERN GOAL

They have allowed supporters from their clubs to travel to Wembley old and new and experience a return journey with feelings infinitely more positive than disappointment and resentment.

The FA Vase Final has been contested 44 times at the time of writing.

The North East has provided a finalist on 15 occasions, with 12 sides bringing the famous trophy back to the region.

One of my favourite moments in putting this book together was interviewing three-time Vase winner Paul Chow.

The former Whitley Bay striker is quite simply a Vase legend having scored for the Seahorses in three consecutive finals between 2009 and 2011.

Occasionally the worlds of football's elite and part-time players meet, even for the briefest of spells.

Chow tells a tale of how he walked into the Wembley dressing room ahead of the 2011 final against Coalville Town.

He saw his number ten shirt hanging up and realised he was sitting in the same seat that Lionel Messi would be sat in just six days later when Barcelona faced Manchester United in that year's Champions League Final.

That story shows the beauty and the essence of what football is all about.

Whilst Messi earns millions upon millions and plays for one of the biggest and most recognisable clubs in the world, Chow works in an office and plays for a Northern League club in front of hundreds, rather than hundreds of thousands.

Their worlds are so far apart but for a few hours they are essentially the same person.

They are both footballers, both goalscorers, carrying the hopes and dreams of those people that hold their clubs close to their hearts.

They hold something else in common – both of them are winners and that is what we celebrate in this book.

The North East has a special bond with the FA Vase and this book tells the stories of some key figures involved in the region's winning teams.

I have been fortunate enough to witness many of the wins at first-hand, whether as a supporter of the region's clubs or sat in Wembley Stadium's press area.

We are lucky to have so many great clubs and personalities involved at this level of the game.

I hope you enjoy reading the tales that are told as much as I enjoyed hearing them and putting them into print.

Mark Carruthers

CHAPTER ONE

1978

WEST END BOY MAKES HISTORY

FA Vase Final 1978

Newcastle Blue Star 2-1 Barton Rovers (at Wembley)

On the day of the Final

Prime Minister: James Callaghan (Labour)

Number One Single

Matchstalk Men and Matchstalk Cats & Dogs (Brian and Michael)

At the Cinema

Dawn of the Dead, The Buddy Holly Story, The End

Football in 1978

World Cup Winners: Argentina
Division One Champions: Nottingham Forest
FA Cup Winners: Ipswich Town
League Cup Winners: Nottingham Forest
European Cup Winners: Liverpool
UEFA Cup Winners: PSV Eindhoven
Cup Winners Cup Winners: Anderlecht
Ballon d'Or Winner: Kevin Keegan (Hamburg)
PFA Player of the Year: Peter Shilton (Nottingham Forest)
FA Trophy Winners: Altrincham
Northern League Winners: Spennymoor United
Northern League Cup Winners: Blyth Spartans
Durham Challenge Cup Winners: Ryhope Colliery Welfare
Northumberland Senior Cup Winners: Blyth Spartans

IAN CRUMPLIN - NEWCASTLE BLUE STAR

On Saturday 11th August 2018 one of the most iconic names in North East non-league football made its return to the game.

A new-look Newcastle Blue Star kicked off their Northern Alliance Premier Division campaign with a home game against Percy Main.

It should be pointed out that the club has no affiliation to the Blue Star that became a staple of North East football for many years before folding in 2009.

It is, in fact, the new name for Alliance club Hazelrigg Victory.

This new Blue Star hosted their North Tyneside opponents at their Scotswood Sports Centre home, a mere mile from where our first FA Vase hero was raised.

Lemington, much like Scotswood, is a working-class village in the heart of Newcastle Upon Tyne's West End.

It is an uncompromising village, with a strong industrial history, where family values and hard graft are common-place amongst the 10,000 people that call Lemington "home".

The village's folk were, up until fairly recently, largely employed at Lemington Glassworks, an unusual cone-shaped building not far from the banks of the River Tyne.

It was a landmark used by German bombers as a turning-point for their regular raids on Newcastle's shipyards and munitions factories during World War Two.

Lemington is famous for little else but it did provide the upbringing for Ian Crumplin, a man that would write his name into the North East's non-league folklore on a historic day at Wembley in 1978.

"Crumpy" had forged a reputation as one of the region's most-feared goalscorers with the likes of North Shields and Ashington.

But it was his move to Wearside League club Newcastle Blue Star that really kicked his career into overdrive and gave him the chance to live out a boyhood dream at the home of English football.

The FA Vase Final of 1978 would be his first and only visit to Wembley, although it wasn't for the lack of trying.

"I had never been to Wembley and I have never been since," explained Crumplin.

"As a Newcastle United fan and a striker for my school team, I idolised the likes of 'Pop' Robson, Wyn Davies and 'Supermac', Malcolm MacDonald.

"I was at every home game of the Fairs Cup run in 1969 and it sealed my love of the game.

"That run made me realise that I wanted to be a footballer and I wanted to score goals.

"I camped out all night to get a ticket for Newcastle's FA Cup Final against Liverpool in 1974.

"My Dad used to go to all of the games, before we were born he went home and away.

"I queued up for hours to get a ticket and my Dad said get just one ticket.

"In my head I am thinking, that's great he's giving it to me.

"But he didn't, he went himself, so that was a bit of a kick in the teeth"

Wembley would have to wait for Crumplin.

After initial success with Ashington, Crumplin was persuaded to join North Shields by another man that has carved his own name in the region's non-league history books.

Jackie Marks was Blyth Spartans assistant manager when the Croft Park club made national headlines by reaching the Fifth Round of the FA Cup in 1978.

He took Crumplin to North Shields where he played alongside two other key figures in Spartans' history-making side – Rob and Steve Carney.

Crumplin found initial success with the Robins, but another Carney would soon end his career at Appleby Park.

"Jackie came banging on my door at my home in Lemington begging me to sign so I did.

"I did well when I went to North Shields, I was scoring goals and enjoying my football.

"But then he left and another bloke came in to replace him.

"He was called Jimmy Carney, he was no relation to Steve and Rob.

"I just couldn't score a goal for him, I went about 15 games without scoring and that was unheard of for me.

"I went to North Shields ahead of pre-season training at the start of my second season and asked when we started.

"Jimmy asked if I had received a letter, which I hadn't.

"Then the letter turned up a few days later and it was basically the club saying they didn't want me"

A brutal way to leave a club but it opened up a whole new chapter in Crumplin's football career.

He stepped away from the Northern League and a move to Newcastle Blue Star was secured but Crumplin experienced a very different club to the one he had left.

Blue Star played in the Wearside League and played in front of small crowds at their Wheatsheaf home.

They had found success on Wearside, winning the league in 1974 and 1976, finishing as runners-up in the year between their two title triumphs.

For Crumplin, the move was about one thing, rekindling his love of the game.

"I just wanted to enjoy my football again and I thought I could do that at Blue Star.

"We had a good side, full of good players.

"The Northern League was a lot stronger at the time and my time there made me even better in the Wearside League.

"I had great players around me as well and I remember the first game we played Whickham, they thought they were the bee's knees.

"Colin Richardson was their manager and everyone in North East non-league football knows about Colin Richardson.

"Whickham were well-known for being physical but they didn't get the respect they deserved for being good players on the ball.

"We played them and I think Colin Richardson thought he had a good side but we butchered them.

"We won 3-0, I scored two but it should have been six or seven.

"We knew we had something special and they must have realised what they were up against.

"It was a perfect start"

The league season soon took a break as focus moved to the FA Vase.

Hertfordshire-based Hoddesdon Town became the inaugural winners of the competition as the Spartan League side secured the Vase with a 2-1 win over Epsom and Ewell in the 1975 final.

Billericay Town were the 1976 winners with a 1-0 win over Stamford and became the first team to retain the Vase, beating Sheffield in a replay at Nottingham Forest's City Ground.

The North East was yet to make an impact in a competition that it would almost monopolise four decades later.

For Crumplin, the competition was a new experience and Wembley was just somewhere that the greats of English football showcased their skills.

He said "Playing in the Northern League, I had never heard of the Vase.

"We went into the first game at Eppleton and people said that the final was at Wembley.

"I thought my new team-mates were having me on if I am honest.

"I remember thinking that non-league just don't get to play at Wembley, that just doesn't happen to us.

"The season before I joined they did pretty well in the competition and it meant that we went into the Vase at the Second Round"

That Second Round draw took Blue Star to their Wearside League rivals Eppleton Colliery Welfare.

The game should have been a comfortable win according to Crumplin but his side were given a serious test and one that could have ended their campaign before it really began.

"Nine times out of ten we would have beaten Eppleton comfortably and that's no disrespect to them," said Crumplin.

"I put us one up midway through the first-half but I have to admit they hammered us after half-time.

"They missed chances and our defence played really well but they must have come off the pitch thinking that they should have won the game.

"We got through that tie and never looked back, it wasn't the last time we could have seen the run ended there and then"

Goals flowed from that point onwards as Blue Star's much-celebrated attacking triumvirate of Paul Dixon, David Callaghan and Crumplin himself teased and tormented Washington and Brigg Town.

Eight goals went past Washington in a thrilling ten-goal game at the Wheatsheaf and Brigg succumbed to a similar fate, going down 8-1 in a replay after a 2-2 draw in Lincolnshire.

That set up a tie against Merseyside-based Prescot Town and the Mid-Cheshire League champions were seen as one of the strongest sides left in the competition.

They provided a stern test of Blue Star's credentials and one that gave Crumplin a first sign that Wembley was clearly in their sights.

"The Prescot game changed everything because they were the best side we faced in the competition.

"It hit home just how tough it was becoming because we drew 2-2 at home and they had a man sent-off.

"Everyone had a feeling that if they could draw against us at our place, with a man sent-off, they would hammer us down there.

"We went down to Merseyside after a bit of a wait because of the snow in the North East.

IAN CRUMPLIN - NEWCASTLE BLUE STAR

"But we got down there and ground out a 1-0 win and their committee told us that we would win the competition because we were that good

"I thought 'wow, that will do for me'"

A thrilling 4-3 home win against Yorkshire League club Frecheville Community sealed a two-legged semi-final against Gloucestershire County League champions Almondsbury Greenway.

Preparations were far from ideal.

Crumplin explained "It was a long journey and it was an unbelievable one.

"We had a bus for the coaches, one for the players and one for the supporters.

"We checked out from the hotel to get to the ground and our bus followed the supporters because they knew where the ground was.

"We lost them so we didn't have a clue where we were going.

"The chairman flagged a local man down and gave him £20 to show us where to go.

"We actually got ready coming off the bus, we didn't have time to warm up for the game.

"Our manager Peter (Feenan) had to do the team-talk on the bus and we just went straight into the game"

Whatever Feenan said clearly made an impact as his side ran out 3-1 winners, an amazing performance after all of the issues that had gone before.

That was one foot in the final and a glorious day at Wembley was secured with a 1-1 draw back in the North East.

Blue Star were on the brink of history and Crumplin had one eye on creating a record of his own.

The striker had scored in every round of the competition so far and one more at Wembley would put him in the history books.

He joked "I was aware of that record but mainly because I kept telling everyone that I had scored in every round.

"I was the laziest player we had but everyone else worked hard to give me the chance to score goals"

Crumplin's chances of making history at Wembley were almost wiped out just a week before the final.

As was the norm at the time, the striker still played Sunday League football and one centre-back was determined to make a name for himself by ending his dreams of a day out at the home of English football

NORTHERN GOAL

"I am a great believer of fate and getting injured didn't cross my mind because of that.

"Peter kept changing the side in the run up to the final to protect us ahead of the game.

"I was playing for Lemington Social Club on a Sunday and we played against a side from Tynemouth on the Sunday before the Vase Final.

"People were saying I was mad for playing but I just wanted to play.

"I walked out of the changing-room and their two big centre-backs got hold of me.

"One of them said that I wouldn't be playing at Wembley because he was going to snap my leg in two.

"What a thing to say!

"They tried to but the manager took me off because it was getting a bit rough but I wanted to stay on and score.

"For someone to say that to you, it's awful now I think about it"

Injury avoided, all eyes turned towards Wembley and a Final against Barton Rovers.

Media attention was ramped up and Crumplin became the centre of attention in Lemington.

"Tyne-Tees Television spoke to us and the Evening Chronicle started doing the same.

"I was walking around Lemington and people were saying they had seen me in the papers.

"It was an unusual experience but I quite enjoyed it if I am honest"

Little was known of their Final opponents but the first meeting between the two sides came on the morning of the big game.

It was clear that there were differences between Blue Star and their rivals.

"We turned up in jeans and t-shirts and they were in suits and ties," said Crumplin.

"People thought I was nervous because I was quiet but I was just taking it all in.

"Someone suggested a walk up the famous stairs to the Royal Box but we decided that we should just leave that for later on when we won the game.

"Barton didn't wait and all of their players walked up the stairs there and then.

"They saw us on the pitch and one of their players pretended to lift the trophy.

IAN CRUMPLIN - NEWCASTLE BLUE STAR

"I remember thinking I hope you only have fresh air between your hands later on mate.

"Not that we needed it, but that was extra-motivation to say the least"

All of Crumplin's goals on the Road to Wembley had been scored wearing the same Adidas boots.

They were in serious need of repair and only a quick trip to a Cobblers on Gosforth High Street saw them fit for the big day at Wembley.

The boots were thrown away at half-time at Wembley as Crumplin struggled to get into the game during the first-half.

The two sides ventured back into the dressing-rooms having scored a goal apiece.

Pete Smith put Rovers ahead on 19 minutes when his cross deceived Blue Star keeper Bobby Halbert.

That lead lasted just five minutes when Barry Dunn produced a sublime chip over the Rovers keeper and future Sheffield United and Leeds United manager Kevin Blackwell.

It was game on but Crumplin always believed that his side would come out on top.

"We weren't great in the first-half and I don't know why.

"They scored a fluke goal, it was a cross and it just sailed over Bobby Halbert's head, hit the far-post and went in.

"We didn't really have time to think about the situation because it was only five minutes later when Barry (Dunn) got the equaliser.

"That was a great time to get back in the game and I think without that, they would have thought they had us.

"We never thought we would get beat, publically we weren't saying it but I remember in the dressing-room we knew we could get the goals to win the game.

"We always scored.

"Paul Dixon, myself and David Callaghan had over 100 goals that season.

"We knew one of us would score"

Blue Star grew in confidence as the second-half wore on.

There was no time for talk of the energy-sapping Wembley pitch or tired legs after a long season.

History beckoned, although it had to wait just a little bit longer after a penalty miss from Jimmy Thomson.

Thomson's spot-kick hit the bar before Crumplin smashed the rebound over from the edge of the box.

His time would come.

There was just one minute left on the clock when it arrived.

Crumplin's replacement boots weren't needed as he netted a rare header.

Even now, memories, movements and noises remain vivid in his mind.

"I didn't score many headers.

"I remember making the run into the box and thinking I hope Peter (Davison) finds me.

"Some of his crosses would end up in the crowd and some were inch-perfect, so you never knew what you were going to get with him.

"I remember their defence was all over the place and I got a running jump and I knew it was going in as soon as I hit it.

"I just ran once it went in, just kept running, it was a blank.

"The lads in the dugout were saying the game was done, I didn't even realise how close it was to the end of the game.

"I just wanted the hear that whistle so I could always say I scored the winning goal at Wembley"

The whistle arrived and Blue Star's immortality was now reality.

Crumplin, the Lemington lad, the Sunday League player, was a history-maker.

There was to be one more moment of comedy upon their return to Tyneside.

The club's main sponsors – Newcastle Breweries – had arranged for a Beer dray to pick up the players from Washington Services in preparation for a parade around Newcastle city centre.

The players clung onto the Vase as they climbed up on the vehicle usually used to transport barrels of beer and made the 15-minute journey into the city centre.

The reception was underwhelming to say the least.

The reception wasn't publicised and the Blue Star players were met by bewildered Sunday shoppers and little else.

That day at Wembley remains Crumplin's sole visit to the Stadium.

He still vows never to return.

"I don't want to go to Wembley again, I have no interest in doing that.

"I have been once, I scored a last-minute winner to win the Vase for my club.

"I should thank Jimmy for missing that penalty but as I have said, I believe in

IAN CRUMPLIN - NEWCASTLE BLUE STAR

fate and I believe I was meant to score the winner that day.

"I never thought after scoring the winner at Eppleton that I would do the same at Wembley.

"Maybe I am blowing my own trumpet here but I was the first player to score a winning goal for a North East club in an FA Vase Final.

"Nobody can ever take that away from me, a lad from Lemington, a proud Lemington lad, it brings a tear to the eye.

"Why would I want to go again because that experience isn't going to be beaten is it?"

CHAPTER TWO

1981

THE WHICKHAM WAY

FA Vase Final 1981

Whickham 3-2 Willenhall Town (A.E.T)

On the day of the Final

Prime Minister

Margaret Thatcher (Conservatives)

Number One Single

Stand and Deliver (Adam and the Ants)

At the Cinema

Graduation Day, Friday 13th Part Two, The Burning

Football in 1981

Division One Champions: Aston Villa
FA Cup Winners: Tottenham Hotspur
League Cup Winners: Liverpool
European Cup Winners: Liverpool
UEFA Cup Winners: Ipswich Town
Cup Winners Cup Winners: Dinamo Tbilisi
Balon d'Or Winner: Karl-Heinz Rummenigge (Bayern Munich)
PFA Player of the Year Winner: John Wark (Ipswich Town)
FA Trophy Winners: Bishops Stortford
Northern League Winners: Blyth Spartans
Northern League Cup Winners: Spennymoor United
Durham Challenge Cup Winners: Horden Colliery Welfare
Northumberland Senior Cup Winners: Blyth Spartans

THE WHICKHAM WAY

It was the Whickham way.

Everyone in it together, us against the world, whatever it takes.

Mental and physical toughness, a spirit that was nurtured by one of North East non-league football's most iconic figures and embraced by the players that followed his every word.

Nobody beats us, nobody breaks us, nobody takes what is ours, whatever that means doing.

The Whickham side were led by the incomparable Colin Richardson, a divisive character to some, but to his players he was everything.

That was something that became clear to Bill Cawthra when he crossed the Tyne to join the club from North Shields.

The prolific striker settled easily into life with Whickham, but his first season was tempered with the fact that his former club Newcastle Blue Star had become the first North East club to lift the FA Vase with a 2-1 win against Barton Rovers.

Not that Cawthra felt any ill-will towards his former team-mates.

He said "It was frustrating in a way, but I had gone from North Shields to Whickham when Blue Star won the Vase in 1978.

"It didn't hurt as much because Whickham were doing so well.

"We won the league that year and I can remember the day of their final.

"We played Chester-le-Street away and the whole dressing-room wanted Whickham to do it, both dressing-rooms actually.

"When the result came through, we all had a pint and celebrated.

"We had progressed ourselves, and we wanted a Wembley final, but there was no negativity towards them.

"The Blue Star lads were my mates, I couldn't have any bitterness towards them."

The same couldn't be said for Richardson, who became obsessed with winning the trophy that his Wearside League rivals had lifted.

The competition was a key target ahead of the 1980/81 season.

Cawthra sensed his manager's desperation to be the next North East club to secure a Wembley win.

"I had left Whickham and played in America for a year and I came back in the back end of the season before we got to Wembley.

"We were doing alright, but we knew we were better.

"I was lucky in a way because I was due to go back to America, but I ended up staying.

NORTHERN GOAL

"The manager, Colin Richardson, was obsessed with winning the Vase.

"But it was only because Blue Star had done it, Colin was obsessed with them and he wanted to win it simply because they had.

"In his head he always wanted the Vase.

"When you are a manager of his class, although some didn't like him, he had this thing where the Vase was the big thing."

There have been many things said and written about Richardson throughout his career.

Cawthra won't have a bad word said about the former Gateshead manager, and pointed to his ability to make a difference in players as a key reason for his success.

"I would say I was one of the lucky ones with Colin because I was a grafter.

"I used to work hard across the front-line and scored goals, so he took a shine to me.

"But, in the same breath, he just loved footballers.

"He loved Micky Carroll, Ian Diamond, Dave Norton.

"He loved footballers.

"Diamond had come from Blue Star and Colin signed him.

"Colin knew something was missing in Ian and he invited him to train on a Tuesday night on his own.

"I asked Ian what happened, and he said he couldn't walk.

"Colin had laid him down by a fence and he had to jump up and attack a ball.

"On the Saturday, he was just a different kid.

"He was tougher and stronger, but that was Colin, he could see something and if you didn't do what he told you, you were gone."

Whickham's Vase game kicked off with a narrow 1-0 win at Stockton Buffs and they progressed into round four with a win by the same score-line against Guisborough Town.

Both games saw Cawthra and his team-mates subjected to a tough, physical challenge, but life in the Wearside League had prepared them for such challenges.

As a Tyneside-based club they had become a target, but out of that came a hardened mentality.

It was Whickham against the world.

"Stockton was the hardest game of the run.

"We played them and then Guisborough Town, but Stockton was the toughest.

"Both games were 1-0 wins and there were chances for both of our opponents.

"We had gone into both games having played three games in a week and it was hard work.

"Then you added training into the mix, and it became even tougher.

"It was a battle, but nobody took the p*ss because we were a tough group and we were used to a battle.

"We were a Tyneside club in the Wearside League, so we knew we would be targeted."

Richardson's steely determination and organisational skills were getting the best out of his side at both ends of the pitch.

Whereas the likes of Cawthra and Ian Diamond were running amok in the final third, the back five were amongst the best at their level in the non-league game.

Disciplined, organised, together.

A trip to Salford saw the Lang Jacks defence left unbreached for a third consecutive Vase tie.

This was the Whickham way that Richardson cherished.

"We were winning games in the Whickham way," laughed Cawthra.

"There is a reason why we didn't concede goals and it was down to Colin.

"Everyone bought into what he wanted, and he rotated quite well, there weren't many complaints.

"He had that presence, even the lads on the line wouldn't leave because we knew something special was coming.

"If he was dropping you there was always a reason.

"He made sense, he knew what he was doing, and we all got behind that.

"We would have run through brick walls for him.

"He could be seen as a horrible man, he went over the line sometimes, but he knew how to get the best out of everyone."

Wembley came into clear focus with a 2-0 home win against a strong Thackley side.

Cawthra was the match-winner and grabbed both goals to see his side through to the last eight of the competition.

Not that he was there to witness the celebrations.

Attempts to secure a memorable hat-trick were ended by a punch to the nose by the Thackley goalkeeper.

That led to a visit to Newcastle's General Hospital, where the striker was given an indication of the impact his side's Vase run was starting to have on Tyneside's football public.

"The first time I realised just how much of an impact we were making was at home against Thackley.

"I had scored two goals and then their keeper broke my nose.

"He said he was trying to punch a ball clear, but he wasn't.

"I went to the General Hospital to get sorted and a doctor came in.

"I still had my black and white shirt on, and he came in and asked my name.

"I told him, and he said that he had just been listening to the game on the radio and congratulated me on getting through.

"It was all a bit strange, but it made me realise that people were paying attention and that we were getting close to Wembley."

Windsor & Eton were stood between Cawthra, Richardson and their dream of a Wembley final.

A two-legged semi-final tie was on the agenda with the away leg first up for the Lang Jacks.

A clinical finish from Cawthra handed his side the perfect start, but an equaliser left the tie in the balance as the two sides prepared to meet on the south bank of the Tyne.

Richardson needn't have worried; his Wembley ambitions were alive and kicking as his side edged a tight contest to secure their place in the final.

"Colin had been to watch them (Windsor & Eton), and he was very thorough.

"I scored early on and I thought here we go.

"They equalised and he was very angry about it, but we had a goal in the tie ahead of the home leg.

"It wasn't a pretty game, far from it.

"They dug in and they had some good players, but then the winner came.

"A ball came in from the right and I was going to head it in, but I saw the defender and keeper coming towards me.

"So, I headed to Paul Allon and he put it in.

"I can remember it like it was yesterday, we had done it and we were on our way to Wembley."

Nothing was left to chance in the preparations for the final.

Richardson's attention to detail paid off as his squad were allowed to continue with their usual pre-match preparations.

A light training session, a pre-match meal and a "couple of pints" on the eve of the game settled down a squad that Cawthra believes could get nervous ahead of the big game with Willenhall Town.

"We met at Whickham and got the bus to Wembley," he explained.

"Colin kept us calm, because we had some strange lads in the squad, and we needed to keep focused.

"I roomed with Ian Diamond at the time and we helped each other.

"We trained at the hotel and prepared on a patch of grass there.

"On the night before the game we had our meal and had a couple of pints before bed.

"It was a normal Friday night and it helped us massively."

Cawthra was an experienced figure in a Whickham squad that had some fresh faces.

Whereas the youngsters failed to grasp the size of their achievements, the striker was taking it all in.

Every last detail of their day in the sun at Wembley is etched on his mind.

"I had been to Wembley for Newcastle United games in 1974 and 1976, but this was different.

"It was a fantastic experience because I had seen my heroes playing there.

"I was breathing everything in.

"I remember getting off the bus, coming into the dressing-rooms and we were looked after so well.

"There were two lads helping us and they were great.

"I remember daft things, like the two of them telling us where the champagne was for full-time.

"The team was revealed, but there wasn't a surprise really.

"We were ready."

The words of Richardson were ringing in the ears of the Whickham players as they stood in the tunnel alongside their final opponents.

"Keep it tight, no daft goals, no mistakes" was the manager's parting-shot to the players he believed would deliver his Vase dream.

The West Midlands outfit took advantage of some surprisingly poor defending from a usually-reliable Whickham defence.

They raced into an early two-goal lead and left Richardson's men with a mountain to climb.

NORTHERN GOAL

Alan Scott halved the deficit, before a cruel twist of fate turned the final in Whickham's favour.

"We were dire in the first 20 minutes," admitted Cawthra.

"There were mistakes, but it was just nerves.

"People were making mistakes that they had never done before.

"They were a good side, but things turned in our favour when I caught their keeper and he had to go off.

"They put a striker in goal, but these are things that happen.

"They wouldn't have shown us any sympathy, so why would we show them any.

"We knew we could do it and we knew we could win the Vase, despite the fact that we were behind.

"We had the mentality, we had the fitness and we were confident."

The belief spread throughout the players as they made their way back on to the hallowed Wembley turf.

This was their time, their moment and they had to do all that they could to grasp it.

They were level just 12 minutes after the restart thanks to a goal from Ronnie Williamson.

Chances came and went, a winner just evaded them.

Extra-time was required.

The Whickham way had to kick in as the energy sapped from the limbs of their players.

In the dying seconds of the first period of extra-time Cawthra, alert as ever, stole possession in a dangerous area and raced in on goal.

He squeezed a shot beyond the advancing keeper and watched as the ball agonisingly crept over the line.

He had his Wembley goal, Richardson had his Vase triumph.

"Ronnie scored a great goal to get us back level and I honestly can't remember them having a chance.

"Ian Diamond was gutted about missing out in the Blue Star final, but that only drove him on, and he was unplayable that day at Wembley.

"He gave a little bit extra because of that, he was scary if I am honest.

"The goal came, and it was down to their centre-back making an error.

"I closed down their defender Fox and he tried to play out from the back.

THE WHICKHAM WAY

"I nicked the ball from him and because their full-backs had pushed on I was in on goal.

"The keeper came out and I touched it past him.

"The ball rolled beyond him and I still don't know why I didn't make sure it had gone in.

"Thankfully it did, and I ran across to the fans to celebrate."

There was to be one more surreal moment for Cawthra to cherish.

The full-time whistle brought emotion and relief.

The post-match celebration brought unexpected visitors into the communal bath.

He explained "The whistle went, and I can remember everything so vividly.

"I remember getting the photos done, I remember the look on the faces of the committee men.

"But the biggest memory was getting in the bath after the game.

"We all jumped in and we were singing and dancing.

"Colin was elated, it was his dream.

"There was one bizarre moment where a Whickham supporter ended up in the dressing-room.

"He ran and jumped in and just disappeared under the water.

"It was typical Whickham, but nobody could take anything away from us."

The Whickham way had prospered on Wembley Way.

CHAPTER THREE

1997

SEASIDERS SUCCESS

FA Vase Final 1997

Whitby Town 3-0 North Ferriby United

On the day of the Final

Prime Minister

Tony Blair (Labour)

Number One Single

Love Won't Wait (Gary Barlow)

At the Cinema

The Fifth Element, The Lost World: Jurassic Park, Austin Powers

Football in 1997

Premier League Champions: Manchester United
FA Cup Winners: Chelsea
League Cup Winners: Leicester City
Champions League Winners: Borussia Dortmund
UEFA Cup Winners: Schalke 04
Cup Winners Cup Winners: FC Barcelona
Balon d'Or Winner: Ronaldo (Inter Milan)
PFA Player of the Year Winner: Alan Shearer (Newcastle United)
FA Trophy Winners: Woking
Northern League Winners: Whitby Town
Northern League Division Two Winners: Northallerton Town
Northern League Cup Winners: Bedlington Terriers
Ernest Armstrong Cup Winners: Jarrow Roofing
Durham Challenge Cup Winners: Spennymoor United
Northumberland Senior Cup Winners: Bedlington Terriers

SEASIDERS SUCCESS

There aren't many more recognisable faces in North East non-league football than that of Harry Dunn.

As a player he found success with Scarborough, winning two FA Trophy winners medals, scoring in their final win against Dagenham in 1977.

A spell with Blyth Spartans was brought to an end in 1983 as he returned to his first club Bishop Auckland.

He seemed a natural leader, quiet and unassuming, but with knowledge and nous that were second-to-none.

A move into coaching and management seemed inevitable.

Dunn explained the reasoning behind his move into the dugout with Bishop Auckland.

He said "Brian Newton was the Bishop Auckland manager at the time, and he invited me to become a coach alongside him.

"I fancied the idea of having a go and I don't know if I would have had a go at a lesser club.

"Bishops were a great club and I enjoyed being there.

"I had a go and I think I did alright.

"I enjoyed being a leader.

"I had from being a boy because I captained my school team, so I became a leader at an early age.

"I captained Ferryhill Juniors and I always liked responsibility.

"I thrived on it."

A short spell in charge of Blyth Spartans was followed by a move down the coast to Whitby Town.

Dunn had forged a strong relationship with the Seasiders committee and the club as a whole during his playing career.

He was appointed as their new manager in December 1995 but faced a challenging first season fraught with on and off-field challenges.

"I always enjoyed going to Whitby Town," explained Dunn.

"Whenever we played there, I loved the place.

"I got to know a few people at the club, and I got on with them very well.

"There came an opportunity to have a go at managing them, I couldn't turn it down and it turned out very well."

"The first year was very difficult on and off the pitch.

"The floodlights were blown down and there was a real risk that the club would be punished for not replacing them.

NORTHERN GOAL

"There was very little money around the place and the town had to rally around us.

"The town's people helped the club take off and they got us back to where we should be.

"We had to reward them with success.

"They gave their hard-earned money and we felt we had to give something back to them.

"It drove us on, and it made us so determined to do something special.

"We didn't get help from any of the authorities, so everyone in and around the club had to work their b*****ks off to try and get us back on our feet.

"People were out and about doing allsorts to raise money.

"We got our just rewards."

Driven on by the spirit of togetherness and generosity, Whitby embarked on a historic 1996/97 season.

Dunn had strengthened his squad with several notable captures and results quickly improved.

The focus was very much on promotion from the Northern League, but an unexpected FA Cup run provided the club with one of the most remarkable ties in the competition's recent history.

Dunn said "It was a one-off season and it will always live with me.

"We had a brilliant FA Cup run and we pushed Hull City all of the way in the first round of the competition.

"We were 4-3 up with 20 seconds left to play and that's how close we were to an upset.

"The referee, Roy Pearson, was from Easington and I have seen him many times.

"He always says 'just 20 seconds Harry'.

"It was one cross and one goal in 20 seconds and that drained us.

"We looked physically and emotionally drained and we ended up getting beat 8-4.

"We weren't sure how we would pick the lads up after that.

"We couldn't let them feel sorry for themselves, and to be fair they were magnificent."

The Seasiders were also preparing to take part in the FA Vase for only the second time in their history.

Their maiden campaign was ended by a 4-1 defeat at Durham City during the

SEASIDERS SUCCESS

previous season.

But this time, they fancied their chances of going far in the competition.

The league was the priority, but there were eyes cast towards a run in the Vase.

"At the time, promotion into the Unibond League was the main target," admitted Dunn.

"We didn't make a great start to the season, we got beat at Tow Law Town on the first day of the season and we had been beaten at Easington in the September.

"That was a turning-point, because we gave them a rocket and the lads reacted.

"The Northern League was a strong league, but we had some good players and we thought we had half a chance in the Vase.

"But there were big-hitters around the country.

"We didn't think we would ever get to Wembley, we knew we needed some luck and a kind draw."

The first two steps on the road to Wembley saw Dunn's side facing familiar opposition in Crook Town and Billingham Synthonia.

Both ties took place at Whitby's Turnbull Ground and were negotiated with narrow wins.

David Logan and Paul Pitman found the target in a 2-1 win at Crook, whilst Synners were beaten by a single Graham Robinson goal.

The hardened nature of the Northern League, coupled with an improved Seasiders squad, had put the club into the third round of the competition.

Dunn said "We knew our first opponents very well, they knew us too.

"We had signed some great players and the squad was looking strong.

"The likes of Andy Toman, Laurie Pearson and Mitch Cook all improved us around the park.

"We had experience and we had football-nous.

"We needed all of that.

"We had a half-decent side and the early-stages were tough.

"It was a really tough competition, every game was difficult and the first two rounds, against other teams from the area, were amongst the toughest games we faced."

Realisation that a tilt at Wembley set in with a trip to Lincolnshire to face Louth United.

NORTHERN GOAL

Whitby were favourites to win the tie and to do so with ease.

Dunn's side were given a stern test, but one that provided him with the realisation that his side were ready for the latter rounds of the competition.

"Louth United away was the moment we thought that Wembley could be a possibility.

"We could have quite easily gone out there, and the game was a bit of a chew on for us.

"It was a banana skin of a tie and we got through in extra-time.

"That was really a routine game, but we learnt how to cope with a game like that because they fought tooth and nail to put us out.

"We showed a different side, we mucked in and got a result in a different way.

"We had the ingredients of a good side and we knew we could go on a good run."

A fifth round home tie against Tiverton Town saw Whitby face a side that Dunn believed were one of the pre-season favourites to lift the Vase.

A tight, nervy affair was played out at the Turnbull Ground, with both sides going for a safety-first approach as they looked to secure a place in the last eight of the competition.

There was to be just one goal, but it fell the way of the Seasiders as Ian Williams found the net to ensure that Dunn's chances of a return to Wembley were kept alive.

"Ian Williams got the goal against Tiverton Town., but we knew they would be tough, we had done our homework on them.

"They were like us.

"If we were away, we would try and just not get beaten.

"They made it really hard for us and it wasn't a great game.

"It was tight, and it was only ever going to be a one-goal game.

"It was edgy, but once we scored there was no way that we were going to let it slip from there."

Dunn's side were rapidly becoming the talk of the town.

Wembley was now just a step away and a two-legged semi-final against Isthmian League side Banstead Athletic was now on the agenda.

Ever the perfectionist, Dunn was meticulous in his approach.

He sought several opinions on the Surrey-based side and made a personal visit to form his own view on their semi-final opponents.

SEASIDERS SUCCESS

The approach paid off.

Laurie Pearson got the only goal of the game in the first leg in Surrey and put his side another step closer to a Vase final.

The second leg, at a packed Turnbull Ground, was tougher and Whitby fell behind.

Their opponents were putting on a much-improved performance after a lacklustre display in the first meeting of the two sides.

Nerves were frayed, chances were missed, extra-time was looming.

But then a chance, a late chance and one that had to be taken.

A long punt into the visitors area fell the way of Paul Pitman and he sent the Seasiders faithful into raptures by lashing the ball into the roof of the net from six yards.

"We got reports on Banstead, and I got to see them too," said Dunn.

"They put it into perspective when their manager said he couldn't believe they were in the semi-final.

"They were halfway up a mediocre lead, but they were solid and organised.

"The local papers had us as red-hot favourites to win, but we knew it wasn't going to be easy.

"Lawrie Pearson got the goal down there and we had a bit of an advantage, but they came to the Turnbull and they were terrific.

"They had us frightened, but we didn't play well.

"If you win away, don't lose your home game, that was what we said.

"The more the game went on, the more tired they got and the more possession we had.

"We were knocking it about, and we should have been more comfortable.

"Their keeper had a stormer and their players were on their knees.

"We grabbed a late goal and we were at Wembley."

There was still work to do in the league campaign, but Dunn's side wrapped up promotion easily by winning all but six of their 38 league fixtures.

The Seasiders were on target for a historic double, and their manager knew that his players needed no warning about their preparations for their big day out at Wembley, where North Ferriby United would be their opponents.

"We had a lot of games to get in before the final and we basically told the players that if they didn't play well in the league, they wouldn't play at Wembley.

"We didn't really have to do that, because the mentality of the team at the time was top-notch.

"We had a great squad and they had the right attitude.

"We shuffled the pack and once the big game comes, we will be ready, and we will go to Wembley as league champions so everyone can focus on having a go there."

Whitby were focused on the big day, but they started slowly.

The Villagers seized the initiative and only several saves from Seasiders keeper Dave Campbell kept the game goalless.

Mark Tennyson went close, Darren France's close-range effort was saved by the feet of Campbell.

Whitby were rocking, but they improved.

Freed from the shackles of their opponent's early dominance, they poured forwards.

David Logan put the Seasiders ahead on the half-hour mark after captain Neil Hodgson had struck the crossbar.

Half-time arrived, Dunn remained calm and cool and summoned up some advice he had been given during his double Wembley win with Scarborough during his playing career.

"They settled quicker than we did," admitted the Seasiders boss.

"They had some good players and they settled down well.

"We had a very good goalkeeper in Dave Campbell, and he kept them out when we were under pressure.

"We knew we would always score, so we weren't worried about being under pressure.

"Logan's goal made it easier at half-time.

"I just told the lads what I had been told when I played at Wembley.

"I just told them to do themselves justice and to do their best in front of their friends and family.

"I asked them all to make a contribution."

The Seasiders players took heed of their manager's advice.

They controlled the second-half and grabbed a second goal on the hour-mark when a stunning drive from Graeme Williams doubled their lead.

A third goal was needed, not to secure the win, but to calm their manager down.

It arrived, much to Dunn's relief, with an acrobatic finish from Andy Toman after Paul Pitman's cross had evaded a crowded area.

SEASIDERS SUCCESS

Dunn made changes, he rewarded his squad for their joint-efforts.

The Vase was theirs to enjoy.

"The second goal wasn't a case of job done, because they had real quality.

"Even at 2-0, we knew that they could get a goal back and put the pressure on us.

"I don't think we would have folded, but we might have folded on the bench.

"We needed another goal and Andy Toman did it with an absolutely terrific goal.

"It was a fantastic goal and that sealed it because they lost a bit of enthusiasm on a big pitch.

"We made changes late on with the game won.

"The most difficult part of the day was picking the starting line-up.

"We got everyone stripped to do the warm-up and then told them the line-up once that was done.

"We wanted everyone involved, this was a whole team effort, and everyone was part of it."

The full-time whistle arrived.

Dunn is well-known for his enthusiasm, but he kept a cool head, wary of how history would reflect on any over-the-top reactions.

The Vase was Whitby's, it was the first time a Northern League club had won the competition.

And Dunn believes that his side's Wembley triumph opened the door for other clubs to match their achievements.

"I just didn't want to make a fool of myself by running around like a scalded cat or a screaming banshee.

"I didn't want to watch it back in ten years' time on television and you are looking like an idiot.

"I enjoyed it, but in a nice way.

"We had said goodbye to the Northern League in a good way and we got messages of goodwill from around the league.

"A lot of them thought if we could do, they could do it.

"We opened the door a little bit.

"The season was a one-off for us, we had an FA Cup run and won a treble.

"It was a remarkable time and I enjoyed every game, it was a special time in my life."

The Northern League was off the mark in the Vase.

CHAPTER FOUR

2002

FATE PREVAILS

FA Vase Final 2002

Whitley Bay 1-0 Tiptree United (A.E.T)

On the day of the Final

Prime Minister

Tony Blair (Labour)

Number One Single

Freak Like Me (The Sugababes)

At the Cinema

About a Boy, The Scorpion King, Spiderman

Football in 2002

Premier League Champions: Arsenal
FA Cup Winners: Arsenal
League Cup Winners: Blackburn Rovers
Champions League Winners: Real Madrid
UEFA Cup Winners: Feyenoord
Balon d'Or Winner: Ronaldo (Real Madrid)
PFA Player of the Year Winner: Ruud Van Nistelrooy (Manchester United)
FA Trophy Winners: Yeovil Town
Northern League Winners: Bedlington Terriers
Northern League Division Two Winners: Shildon
Northern League Cup Winners: Durham City
Ernest Armstrong Cup Winners: Prudhoe Town
Durham Challenge Cup Winners: Bishop Auckland
Northumberland Senior Cup Winners: Bedlington Terriers

FATE PREVAILS

Do you believe in fate?

Are some things just meant to be?

Ian Chandler could probably be put up as a good argument for that being the case.

The man that would go on to become synonymous with both Whitley Bay and the FA Vase could have taken a very different career path before arriving at Hillheads.

Where would the club have been had he secured a shock move to Switzerland?

Or taken an offer from a club in the top-level of the non-league game?

Or decided to leave when his heart seemed set on it?

Maybe some things are just meant to be and Chandler was fated to become one of the most important figures in the club's long history.

As a young striker, he joined Barnsley in the early-1980s and was managed by Leeds United legend Alan Clarke.

It was a brutal introduction into life in professional football, but one that would stand him in good stead throughout his career.

"It was a very different time," explained Chandler.

"The days at Barnsley were brilliant.

"We would be in for training at 10 o'clock, out on the pitch at half-past, finish at half past 12 and then be straight across at the shop for a sausage sandwich.

"Then it was a case of playing pool in the clubhouse at 2 o'clock and you'd just flitter the day away after that.

"Nowadays it's all about video analysis and different tests.

"But it was a great introduction to the game, and I played with the likes of John Beresford and Steve Agnew.

"Alan Clarke was the manager and he would train with us in sandshoes in the rain, but he would never fall over.

"He was still a very good player and he helped me a lot."

Chandler broke into the first-team and was handed a very early return to his native North East.

In only his second start for Barnsley, he was pitched into a battle with Gary Bennett as the Tykes faced Sunderland at Roker Park.

It was a night of contrasting emotions for the young striker.

"My second ever game was at Roker Park against Sunderland.

NORTHERN GOAL

"I had played at Shrewsbury on the Saturday before and did quite well, so Clarke kept me in the team.

"We played at Roker Park and got beat in the League Cup.

"George Burley, Gary Bennett and Shaun Elliott played for Sunderland and I am fairly sure Benno gave me a kick or two throughout the game.

"Ian Hesford played in goal for them too.

"We got to a penalty shoot-out and he saved my penalty.

"I wasn't expecting to take a penalty and I had my boots off.

"I was the nineteenth person to take a penalty, it was a bit of a marathon shoot-out, but we went out after it all."

Chandler spent the 1988/89 season with Aldershot, before returning to the North East in search of a club.

But his planned return was almost interrupted by an unexpected offer to play in Europe.

A move never came to pass, and Whitley Bay fought off several other clubs to hand Chandler his first experience of the non-league game.

"I was playing at Aldershot and an agent asked me to go to Switzerland at the end of the season.

"Aldershot was a funny place, it was a fair way away from the North East.

"They had no reserve team and because of that I couldn't get fit and back into the team once I had an injury.

"This agent said do you fancy going abroad so I ended up going to Grasshoppers in Zurich.

"I had a trial, but I wasn't their style of player.

"I had trials with Newcastle Blue Star and scored, then I trained with Gateshead and a couple of Northern League teams.

"Whitley Bay came out of the woodwork and offered me £20 more than Gateshead.

"I knew a few players like Paul Walker and Kevin Todd."

Chandler settled well at Hillheads and he was part of a Bay side that made national headlines in the FA Cup.

A Preston North End side managed by former Newcastle United star John McGrath and featuring former Magpies midfielder Ian Bogie were beaten in front of the BBC cameras in a second-round tie.

"The squad was very high quality and it felt like a professional squad.

"We had a great run to the third round of the FA Cup, and we beat

FATE PREVAILS

Scarborough, who were a Football League club.

"The famous one was beating Preston North End, and then we fell foul of Rochdale in the Third Round.

"We were playing on Match of the Day, I'd left a pro club to join a non-league club and here I was playing on Match of the Day facing people like Ian Bogie.

"They were great days and laid the foundations for what followed."

The club returned to the Northern League ahead of the 2000/01 season and played in the FA Vase for the first time in their history.

An away defeat at Tow Law Town meant that their maiden campaign was ended in round two of the competition.

That also meant that there was no expectation ahead of their next Vase venture.

Chandler explained "We had a decent run in the FA Cup in the year before and got to the last qualifying round, so there was talk of trying to do that again.

"But the Vase wasn't really discussed.

"We seemed to play the Vase and FA Cup on alternate weekends, but the focus was always on the cup.

"We played Colne early on in the Vase and it was just another game.

"We sneaked through and I got the only goal, but there wasn't any expectation.

"I had never heard of the Vase if I am honest."

Whitley Bay ran a gauntlet of North East clubs in rounds one, two and three.

Dunston Fed, Guisborough Town and Billingham Town were all dispatched to help set up a fourth round tie against Milton Keynes City.

Chandler was left out of the side and had to make do with a place on the bench.

He decided he wanted to leave Hillheads, not that his manager knew anything about it.

"Andy (Gowens) had left me out for the Milton Keynes game, and I wasn't happy," he admitted.

"Far from it in fact.

"I was named as a substitute and I had spoken to Gary Middleton to tell him I was planning to leave.

"I was 33, I couldn't keep coming on as a substitute.

NORTHERN GOAL

"I needed to play football on a regular basis.

"I was dead-set on going but he talked me out of it.

"I came on and scored and I got in the side after that.

"I was just fed up with football, but it all turned around after that game.

"Andy won't even know about that now, well he might if he reads this."

Brigg Town were beaten after a fifth round replay and a hard-earned 2-1 win at Clitheroe put the Bay into the last four of the competition.

They would meet a familiar opponent over two legs for a place in the final.

"We got drawn against Durham City in the semi-final and I didn't mind who we played really.

"Steve Cuggy had spat his dummy out over not being selected and had left the club.

"I still don't know the full story behind it, but he didn't turn up for the first-leg.

"I was playing against Dickie Ord and I thought I did ok.

"We won 2-1 at home and we were preparing for the second game at their place.

"I was under the weather ahead of the game and we knew a draw would see us through.

"I was on my own up front with Michael Fenwick floating around.

"Cuggy had come back into the fold and I was taken off after 65 minutes.

"It was a boring game, there were no goals, but we saw it out and we were through to the final.

"It wasn't pretty, it wasn't exciting, but we were through."

The Football Association had announced that the final was to be played at Villa Park for a second consecutive year with the new Wembley still under construction.

The old stadium had hosted every FA Vase final since 1975, with Football League venues hosting replays on four separate occasions.

There was some disappointment amongst the Bay squad that they would not get a chance to run out at the home of English football.

But Chandler revealed that there was no let-up in the fight for places in the final.

"We were disappointed, a lot of us were.

"Wembley was being redeveloped, but it was a dream to play there.

"It was a small disappointment and, although playing at Villa Park was great,

FATE PREVAILS

it wasn't quite what Wembley would have been for the lads.

"We still all played for our places and there was no slacking off.

"We all wanted to play in the final, but it took something away that it wasn't at Wembley"

Eastern Counties League club Tiptree United stood in the way of Whitley becoming only the fourth club to bring the FA Vase back to the region.

Newcastle Blue Star, Whickham and Whitby Town had triumphed over the past 22 years, and Whitley were determined to add their name to the list.

They started well and were handed a golden chance to take the lead when they were awarded a penalty.

The chance was squandered.

"We had missed a penalty, but we were on top.

"Andy Bowes had a penalty saved and he was unfortunate to be the one that missed it.

"A few months later it appeared on the web that I had missed it.

"I wish I had taken it, I would have scored!"

The game ventured into extra-time and Whitley were building momentum.

With just seven minutes of additional time gone, Chandler had his first real chance of the game.

Cuggy burst down the right and swung a cross into the area, hoping to find the tall forward.

Chandler didn't let his team-mate down, beating a Tiptree defender to the ball and arcing a header beyond the keeper from around 12 yards from goal.

A celebration was planned, but tiredness meant it was hastily abandoned.

Chandler said "There was a feeling the goal was coming.

"There was 97 minutes gone, I still remember the time.

"I hadn't played that many minutes all season.

"The joke was that I should have been off by then, given how old I was by that point.

"Cuggy jokes that he bounced it off my head, but it was a good header, I still say that.

"Everything slowed down as the ball came in.

"I knew all I had to do was get ahead of the defender because I had read what Cugs was going to do.

"I made a lovely contact and it flew in.

NORTHERN GOAL

"It was a good distance from goal, so I think I did well to get one in.

"I was getting called the flat-fish at the time, so I planned to run to the dugout and they would squirt me with water so I could flap around like a fish.

"I couldn't be bothered running that far, so I just lay down and celebrated."

Both sides were wilting in the Villa Park heat and chances were few and far-between and the clock crept its way towards the 120th minute.

Led by their experienced frontman, Whitley saw out time and the final whistle brought scenes of unbridled joy from the men in blue and white.

They had won the competition that nobody seemed bothered about some nine months earlier.

"The Vase wasn't the priority, we always said that," explained Chandler.

"We wanted to win the league and the Vase was a lesser competition.

"There wasn't much money in it.

"But as a player it wasn't really talked about.

"But it certainly was afterwards."

And Chandler would have Whitley Bay talking about the Vase again.

It was just meant to be.

Newcastle Blue Star 1978 CREDIT PAUL DIXON

Billy Cawthra meets Sir Matt Busby ahead of the final 1980 CREDIT WHICKHAM

Billy Cawthra scores the winner for Whickham 1980 CREDIT WHICKHAM

Harry Dunn celebrates on the pitch CREDIT NEIL THALER

Whitby Town celebrate their Wembley win in 1997 CREDIT NEIL THALER

CHAPTER FIVE

2009

THE INSPIRATION

FA Vase Final 2009

Whitley Bay 2-0 Glossop North End

On the day of the Final

Prime Minister

Gordon Brown (Labour)

Number One Single

Number 1 (Tinchy Stryder featuring N-Dubz)

At the Cinema

Star Trek, Angels and Demons, X-Men Origins - Wolverine

Football in 2009

Premier League Champions: Manchester United
FA Cup Winners: Chelsea
League Cup Winners: Manchester United
Champions League Winners: Barcelona
UEFA Cup Winners: Shakthar Donetsk
Balon d'Or Winner: Lionel Messi (Barcelona)
PFA Player of the Year Winner: Ryan Giggs (Manchester United)
FA Trophy Winners: Stevenage Borough
Northern League Winners: Newcastle Benfield
Northern League Division Two Winners: Horden Colliery Welfare
Northern League Cup Winners: Newcastle Benfield
Ernest Armstrong Cup Winners: Horden Colliery Welfare
Durham Challenge Cup Winners: Billingham Synthonia
Northumberland Senior Cup Winners: Newcastle United Reserves

THE INSPIRATION

It was just a normal, uninspiring pre-season friendly.

Multiple substitutions, managers trying out new tactics ahead of the new season, no fluidity, little interest and a game rapidly stagnating in the mid-summer sun as full-time approached.

But for Mark Taylor, it was the start of a life-changing series of events.

Just months earlier, the Whitley Bay full-back had helped the Seahorses become only the fourth North East side to win the FA Vase with a 2-0 victory against Glossop North End.

Taylor had put in a typically energetic display at Wembley, full of effort and commitment.

But here, at St James Park, home of Alnwick Town, a world away from the famous arch of Wembley, something was very different.

Taylor's first-touch and passes weren't up to standard, wrist and ankle injuries suffered during the previous season had failed to clear up and they were affecting his job as a PE teacher.

His form dipped and he started to play for Whitley Bay's reserve team, before returning to train with his former team-mates two months later.

It didn't go well.

Taylor explained "Pre-season quickly came around and I still didn't feel right, but again put it down to the injury and a lack of sharpness.

"We played a friendly at Alnwick Town and I was ok when it came to running, but my touch and passing were horrendous.

"Even worse than normal.

"I slowly got worse and was playing for the reserves and was really struggling.

"In October I trained with the first team and was s**t.

"I got battered by the lads."

Taylor's issues stretched way beyond struggling on the football pitch.

He was to receive some horrendous news.

"I started tripping up and my hand was struggling to write," he explained.

"I realised something was wrong and, as you do, googled my symptoms and one of the outcomes was ALS, or what I later found out is what the Americans call Motor Neurone Disease.

"I paid privately to go to the Nuffield Hospital and they did some tests and said quite plainly that something could be seriously wrong, and they would admit me to hospital after Christmas.

"On the way home from the appointment I rang my girlfriend and asked her

NORTHERN GOAL

to go to my mums who didn't know how much I had been struggling."

Taylor underwent several tests to offer a more conclusive diagnosis, although kept his problems away from his Whitley Bay team-mates.

A trip and slurred speech on a team night out over Christmas were put down to drink, but Taylor knew differently.

Once the festive period had subsided, he was taken into Newcastle's General Hospital for yet more tests.

He didn't need to be told of the outcome, because deep down, he already knew.

"It's a strange feeling sitting hoping that you have a brain tumour, because at least they can do something about it, but deep down I knew it was MND.

"I had loads of visitors including most of the team, which kept my spirits up, but on the fourth day I was called to the doctor.

"He said that all tests indicated that I had MND.

"I asked for him to tell me straight, so he did.

"He said it would be likely that I would be in a wheelchair in six months and the average life expectancy was three years.

"I just thought f**k, how am I going to tell my family that nine months earlier I had the privilege of playing at Wembley for my home town club, but now I would be in a wheelchair in the same amount of time and dead in three years."

Taylor had experienced frustration and anger during his football career.

But this was different, this was life-changing.

This was a kick in the balls, rather than kicking one around a pitch.

Two years earlier there was disappointment in the Vase, but nothing that hit like this.

Taylor had been a squad member when Whitley Bay won their first FA Vase Final with a 1-0 win over Tiptree United at Villa Park.

But now the final was at Wembley and Taylor wanted to get there and experience the cup final experience he had long dreamt of.

It was now within sight.

Whitley reached the semi-final and were paired with Lowestoft Town for a two-legged last-four tie.

A 4-0 defeat in Suffolk was a severe blow that Taylor and his team-mates could not recover from, despite a heroic attempt in the home-leg where they came within one goal of forcing the tie into extra-time.

The defeat was to turn into an inspiration once their next Vase run got

THE INSPIRATION

underway in the early-stages of the following season.

Taylor explained "It was a huge disappointment to lose 4-0 at Lowestoft.

"The early goal, the farcical second goal when I was kicked in the head splitting it open, the sending off of Brian Rowe, then the late fourth meant we were really up against it at home.

"But such was our mentality we still thought we had a chance.

"We so nearly pulled off a monumental comeback, but it wasn't to be.

"After the quarter-final game against Biggleswade Town in 2009, Lowestoft were still in the draw.

"Most of the lads wanted to avoid them, but me and Steve Cuggy had a conversation saying we definitely wanted them in the semi-finals.

"We wanted revenge."

Ian Chandler's side had already seen off Abbey Hey, Penrith, Bootle and Stratford Town to set up their quarter-final home tie against Biggleswade Town.

The Bedfordshire outfit were swept aside as Lee Kerr and Paul Chow were amongst the scorers in a 5-2 win.

The whole squad awaited the draw, it was to be the reunion that Taylor had wanted.

The reaction was immediate, and the Bay gave themselves a chance with a 2-1 win at home in the first-leg thanks to goals from their dynamic duo Kerr and Chow.

But the away leg was to prove a far tougher task.

"When we drew Lowestoft, every one of the lads stepped up their performance in games and training to make sure we were ready for them.

"In the first leg, at home, we were excellent and won 2-1, but it really should have been more.

"In the second leg at their place it was a different game.

"Whitley never do things the easy way and we conceded an early goal.

"But we were always good at set-pieces and Leon Ryan popped up with a bullet header from a corner.

"Davey Coulson turned to me and Pickers (Lee Picton) and shouted that there is no f*****g way we are conceding another f*****g goal, and we didn't.

"Most of the lads had been in the semi-final in the previous year and there was no way we were going to have that feeling again."

Time ticked on, slowly, or so it seems.

NORTHERN GOAL

Questions were asked of the referee, Taylor was almost booked for doing so.

Why hadn't he blown the whistle? When is he going to? Is he even going to?

Just blow the b****y whistle, will you?

"I almost got booked for asking the ref how long was left," admitted Taylor.

"After what seemed like an eternity the whistle finally blew.

"At first the only emotion I felt was relief.

"Then when my family and the fans started running on the pitch the celebration started, and everyone was singing "Tell me ma, me ma".

"We had done it, we were going to play at Wembley."

The Bay squad didn't have to look far for inspiration of what could be achieved in a Vase final.

Their own manager Ian Chandler had grabbed the winner in the 2002 final win against Tiptree and made himself a club legend in doing so.

He was someone to look up to, not least for his former team-mate Taylor.

He said "I first joined Whitley Bay in July 2001 as a seventeen-year-old.

"It was my first season in the Northern League, and I was playing alongside Chan and Cuggs (assistant manager Steve Cuggy).

"I didn't really appreciate how big the Vase was, although I played a part in most of the early rounds, I didn't play much in the last few rounds.

"I broke my foot in the last league game at Dunston, so wouldn't have played in the final anyway.

"I think the fact that I had developed a good relationship with Chan, and Cuggs helped their management of me.

"I wasn't the best player, but I always worked my a**e off and gave 100%.

"I think and hope they knew that they could rely on me.

"He had a knack of attracting the right players to fit in with the team and he motivated us, which is why we had so much success.

"He, and the team had little patience for big time Charlies, apart from Robbo (Paul Robinson) and Leon (Ryan), the team came first."

Taylor was all set for his Wembley date, but there was a league campaign to finish.

An injury suffered in a top of the table clash with Spennymoor Town put his place in the final squad in jeopardy.

"The main memories of the lead up to the final were panic.

THE INSPIRATION

"We played a top of the table clash at Spenny and I went in for a tackle and felt my ankle give way.

"It was about five weeks before the final and obviously I was worried about if I would be fit.

"I also had been having problems with my right hand after falling a couple of months earlier, but I had no idea what those signs meant for me.

"I did everything possible to get fit, icing it, going in the sea and doing my rehab exercises.

"It stopped hurting, but it still didn't feel right or stable and I had to play in the last league game of the season away to Ashington to prove my fitness and guarantee I would start in the final.

"I played the whole game mostly using my left foot, so I was surprised no one noticed as it was mainly for standing on.

"We comfortably won the game and lots of players were rested, even Cuggy played and scored.

"My family were the only people that knew that I wasn't right, and they were so relieved that I had made it."

Whitley were favourites going into the final against Glossop North End and confidence was high amongst the squad.

The big day arrived, and Taylor got his first experience of Wembley.

He explained "It was absolutely boiling hot, probably in the mid-thirties I reckon, but the crowd were amazing with the Bay fans outnumbering Glossop by a few thousand."

The game went to plan.

Whitley lived up to their favourites tag as Kerr and Chow grabbed a goal in each half to ease their side to victory.

The celebrations got underway and Taylor found himself in the media spotlight.

"Despite them hitting the bar and, creating a few half chances, we were very comfortable and never thought we would lose.

"I remember when the full-time whistle was blown, I jumped straight on Davey Coulson to celebrate and then went to look for my family in the crowd just to see them.

"Dicka (former FA Vase winner Paul Dixon) from Radio Newcastle, who I had known for years playing with his son as a kid, grabbed me for an interview.

"I have no idea what I said, I was so caught up in the moment."

"In the changing rooms we cracked open the crates of Carlsberg and started

49

taking photos with the Vase.

"We were laughing and joking, mostly about Moorsey's (Chris Moore) dancing.

"The bus journey home was a long one, most of which was spent by myself asleep on the floor next to the toilet so I could be sick.

"I managed to pull myself round to go to St James' Park to be presented to the crowd at half-time and get a reception from the club, which was such a nice touch.

"Overall, it was a surreal but unforgettable weekend."

Whitley Bay would return to Wembley twelve months later and they would retain the Vase with a comprehensive win against Wroxham.

Taylor was in attendance, but his involvement was limited to that of a supporter after his diagnosis with Motor Neurone Disease.

He was an inspiration to the Whitley Bay class of 2010 and continues to be an inspiration to many with his fund-raising efforts and positivity.

That is why he is held in such high-esteem by his former team-mates.

The feeling is reciprocated.

"Ever since I was diagnosed everyone, the players and fans, have been amazing and supported me in any way they could.

"At the 2010 Vase Final everyone wore t-shirts saying, "Taylor is Mr Effective", which was a bit of a p**s-take as they used to say I had no ability but I was always effective.

"I was really touched that they did that and asked me to lift the Vase.

"The week after that final, the club put on a testimonial for me in a game between the current squad and the 2002 squad.

"About 800 people turned up, which was absolutely amazing, and we raised a load of money.

The fund-raising continues to this day and so too does Taylor's relationship with his former team-mates and friends.

It is a bond forged on the pitch, nourished through success and that has prospered in adversity.

"Over the years I have run loads of events like auctions, talk-ins and football matches, which the lads have always participated in.

"I still keep in regular contact with a group of the local lads and always bump into or get messages asking how I am.

"I think it represents how close we were as a team, which got us through a lot of tough times and made us successful.

THE INSPIRATION

"It has really meant a lot to me how much the players and fans have supported me.

"Despite everything I feel very lucky for that."

CHAPTER SIX

2010

WHEN WORLDS COLLIDE

FA Vase Final 2010

Whitley Bay 6-1 Wroxham

On the day of the Final

Prime Minister

Gordon Brown (Labour)

Number One Single

Good Times (Roll Deep)

At the Cinema

Iron Man 2, Robin Hood, Shrek Forever After

Football in 2010

Premier League Champions: Chelsea
FA Cup Winners: Chelsea
League Cup Winners: Manchester United
Champions League Winners: Inter Milan
Europa League: Atletico Madrid
Balon d'Or Winner: Lionel Messi (Barcelona)
PFA Player of the Year Winner: Wayne Rooney (Manchester United)
FA Trophy Winners: Barrow
Northern League Winners: Spennymoor Town
Northern League Division Two Winners: Stokesley Sports Club
Northern League Cup Winners: South Shields
Ernest Armstrong Cup Winners: Whitehaven
Durham Challenge Cup Winners: Billingham Synthonia
Northumberland Senior Cup Winners: Whitley Bay

WHEN WORLDS COLLIDE

Football has an almost unique quality of bringing people together.

It delivers shared experiences, even in the most unexpected places.

That is one of the most wonderful aspects of the FA Vase.

Normal folk ply their trade on a pitch where multi-millionaire footballers wave their magic wand.

Paul Chow knows that only too well, because he has stood in the place where one of football's greatest magicians prepared for his own Wembley date.

The 2010 FA Vase Final saw the Whitley Bay striker's world collide with who he regards as the greatest player of all-time.

Chow explained "I walked into the changing-room ahead of the 2010 final and looked at my seat, with my number ten shirt hanging up.

"Then it dawned on me.

"The following weekend was the Champions League Final and Barcelona were playing Manchester United at Wembley.

"Here I was, a Northern League striker, sitting in the dressing-room where Barcelona's stars would be getting ready for their big game.

"I couldn't get it out of my head.

"Then I had another thought, I was wearing number ten and Lionel Messi would be too.

"I was sitting in the seat where he would be sitting seven days later.

"It was all numbered, he would be sitting there, the greatest player of all-time.

"That's the magic of Wembley."

Chow hadn't really experienced "the magic of Wembley" in the past, not even on an unusual "flying" visit.

He said "I had been to the old Wembley as a supporter, four times in fact.

"Three as a Newcastle United fan, once as an England supporter.

"I had never seen a goal scored for the team I wanted to score.

"I saw England draw 0-0 with Bulgaria and Newcastle got beat every time I was there.

"In the year before we reached our first final in 2009, I got a bit of a Wembley experience.

"We got beat against Lowestoft Town in the semi-final and I was due to work in Lisbon on the day of the final.

"My plane flew over Wembley when the game was going on and all I could think about was that we should have been there.

"It ruined the weekend and I thought we would never get there."

Whitley Bay headed into the 2009/10 season as FA Vase holders after their 2-0 win against Glossop North End in the previous year's final.

The win was a "wake-up call" for Northern League clubs according to Chow.

"The Vase is the pinnacle for clubs at our level.

"We started the precedent of getting to Wembley and we made Northern League clubs realise just how achievable it was for them.

"The 2009 win was a wake-up call, I think.

"It was seen as a dream before that, but now it was all about getting to Wembley."

A second Wembley appearance had been secured in testing circumstances.

Whilst wins over Alsager Town, Boldmere St Michaels and Poole Town were relatively straightforward, the Seahorses needed two attempts at seeing off Chertsey Town in the fifth round.

That set up a quarter-final tie against Northern League rivals Shildon and fortune favoured Chow and his team-mates.

"That year had been the hardest route to the final.

"We played Chertsey Town away and we beat them with ten men for over half an hour.

"It was tough, it went to extra-time and we got through because we felt they were scared of us.

"We beat Shildon, we probably shouldn't have beaten them, but Phil Brumwell got sent-off and it changed the game."

A stern test awaited Whitley in the last four of the competition and a long trip to Leicestershire was on the agenda.

Barwell were the opposition and they came closer than anyone to ending Chow's dreams of a second appearance at Wembley.

An injury meant he had to watch his side go 3-1 down with the first-leg heading into its last 10 minutes.

Desperation saw Chandler throw his top scorer into the action in the hope of getting a goal back to give them a chance at Hillheads a week later.

He got the goal, and then some.

"We played Barwell in the semi-final," explained Chow.

"I was injured against Newcastle United Reserves a few weeks earlier and I just couldn't get fit.

WHEN WORLDS COLLIDE

"I tried everything, and I was put on the bench.

"David Coulson had to come off injured, Chan asked me to give him something for 10 minutes because we were 3-1 down.

"I scored twice with my only two touches and I knew I wasn't fit.

"I remember the line-up for the second-leg and their captain said that he hoped I had used all of my luck up last week.

"They went ahead early on and it was a hell of a game, but Paul Robinson won it with a header.

"He still talks about it now, in fact he never shuts up about it."

The big day arrived, Norfolk outfit Wroxham stood in the way of Whitley Bay's quest to retain the Vase.

Wembley was basked in sunshine, just as it had been twelve months earlier when they saw off Glossop North End.

A lesson had been learnt that day.

"We learnt from the first year," said Chow.

"It was a boiling hot day against Glossop North End and this one was the same.

"Wroxham warmed-up outside, but Chandler made us warm-up inside where it was cool.

"We were here to win the game, and nothing was left to chance.

"We went in a huff with him to be honest, we just wanted to get out and kick balls into the net and wave at our families.

"But we stretched off indoors, then went out and did a warm-up.

"By that time, they had been out there for half an hour and they were sweating.

"I think that played a big part."

Whitley had suffered a blow in the early part of the season when 2009 finalist Mark Taylor was diagnosed with Motor Neurone Disease less than six months after walking out at Wembley.

The impact on the squad was obvious, but it also provided them with further inspiration to go and win the Vase again.

That was the message from manager Chandler ahead of the game.

Chow revealed "One of the talks in the pre-match was about doing it for Mark.

"We had t-shirts printed with a message for him too.

"It was devastating to see one of our team-mates from the previous year going through what he was going through.

"It was just twelve months, and everything had changed.

"He was an inspiration and we wanted to give him something to enjoy."

Taylor was given something very special to enjoy as he watched on from the Wembley stands.

Within 21 seconds his side were ahead, and it was Chow that wrote himself in the history books with the quickest Wembley goal of all-time.

Not that he could believe he had struck so early in the game.

"It was 21 seconds, even though at Wembley they said 19.

"I have always been a striker and if a keeper spilled the ball I have to be there.

"Leon Ryan played a long ball, it bounced between their defence and keeper, so I went in there.

"They hesitated and I got in there and scored.

"I didn't realise how quick it was, I was worried.

"Nobody scores that quickly at Wembley, I thought something was wrong and that they would rule it out.

"Glen Martin, our physio, told me at half-time that it was the quickest goal at Wembley.

"It didn't mean much then, we had a game to win.

"Even the press lads, Steve Brown and Lee Ryder, they kept telling me at full-time, that's when it hit me."

It was the perfect start.

But Wroxham hit back with a rare attack on 12 minutes.

Bay keeper Terry Burke managed to keep out a header from Paul Cook, but the rebound fell back to the Wroxham striker and he made no mistake at the second attempt.

There was no panic from a Bay side full of character and spirit.

They were back ahead within four minutes when Andy Easthaugh found his own net and Lee Kerr extended the lead less than 60 seconds into the second-half with a typically clinical finish.

Chow turned provider just before the hour-mark when he found Adam Johnston, who made no mistake to make it 4-1.

Chow's number went up just after Johnston's goal and he was replaced by Phil Bell.

It gave him time to reflect on the job he had done and what the day meant

WHEN WORLDS COLLIDE

to those around him.

He said "They equalised, but it didn't worry us, it wasn't a setback.

"It was a case of so what, that was their moment of glory.

"We just knew we were better, and we knew we would keep creating.

"An own-goal got us back ahead and then Lee Kerr scored early in the second-half.

"I think it felt like job done then, but we just wanted more and more.

"I came off just after Adam Johnston had scored our fourth and it gave me a chance to take everything in.

"I didn't really want to come off, I was gutted.

"But then I think about looking around Wembley, to our fans, to my family and it meant the world to me.

"It was a surreal experience, being so laid back, so relaxed at a stadium like that."

Late goals from Paul Robinson and Josh Gillies put a shine on a remarkable performance.

The 6-1 score-line was the biggest FA Vase Final win since Billericay Town's 4-1 win against Almondsbury Gateway in 1978.

It was also the first time any side had scored six times in a Vase final.

But being the goalscorer that he is, Chow was still left with an uncomfortable feeling.

"There were a few times that season we scored five or six, but to do it at Wembley was amazing.

"I was disappointed though.

"How did I only get one of them?

"If we scored six, I would expect to get three of them.

"But it was nice to share the goals around, I suppose."

There were emotional scenes as the Seahorses were presented with the Vase for the second time in 12 months.

Just as he had a year earlier, Mark Taylor was there alongside his team-mates.

He had played as big a role off the pitch in 2010 as he had with a whole-hearted display on it 12 months earlier.

He had inspired his side with his bravery and courage as he began his battle with Motor Neurone Disease.

NORTHERN GOAL

He made his way to the famous Royal Box to celebrate the win with the rest of the Bay players.

It meant a lot to everyone involved with the club, not least Chow himself.

"Mark got the lift up and he was helped up the last flight of stairs.

"To see him there, at Wembley, alongside us, that meant everything.

"More than the goals, more than the record, more than the win even.

"He was a big part of it all for us."

To end this tale, we fast forward to a midweek night in February 2018.

Chow – by this time a Hebburn Town player – had just finished training and was ready for home.

Numerous messages came through on his phone as he got into his car and prepare for the short drive back to his house.

His record had gone, former team-mates were only too happy to inform him.

"I was training with Hebburn Town and it was about nine o'clock.

"I got in the car after training and checked my phone because Newcastle were playing that night.

"I had a load of texts, one from Robbo (Paul Robinson), and a load of tweets too.

"I knew the record had gone.

"I tweeted Eriksen asking for a signed shirt, but he never got back to me.

"It's a fantastic record to have had at one point.

"It's still the quickest cup final goal, Eriksen can't take that one away from me.

"Not yet anyway."

CHAPTER SEVEN

2011

THREE AND NOT SO EASY

FA Vase Final 2011

Whitley Bay 3-2 Coalville Town

On the day of the Final

Prime Minister

David Cameron (Conservative)

Number One Single

Party Rock Anthem (LMFAO)

At the Cinema

The Artist, Drive, Pirates of the Caribbean: On Stranger Tides

Football in 2011

Premier League Champions: Manchester United
FA Cup Winners: Manchester City
League Cup Winners: Birmingham City
Champions League Winners: Barcelona
Europa League Winners: Porto
Balon d'Or Winner: Lionel Messi (Barcelona)
PFA Player of the Year Winner: Gareth Bale (Tottenham Hotspur)
FA Trophy Winners: Darlington
Northern League Winners: Spennymoor Town
Northern League Division Two Winners: Newton Aycliffe
Northern League Cup Winners: Newcastle Benfield
Durham Challenge Cup Winners: Gateshead Reserves
Northumberland Senior Cup Winners: Newcastle United Reserves

THREE AND NOT SO EASY

This wasn't the rough and tumble of the Northern League.

It wasn't the difficult environment that visits to Shildon or West Auckland Town could offer.

The pitch didn't provide a unique challenge with unexpected bobbles and bounces.

This was manicured carpet-like grass, with international stars caressing passes that were asking to be controlled.

This was the dream, this was an opportunity, this could be the start of something big.

But it was unexpected.

This was years before Jamie Vardy began his crawl up the league pyramid from Stocksbridge Park Steels to Leicester City via Halifax Town and Fleetwood Town.

In February 2006, Whitley Bay's 19-year-old striker Lee Kerr was offered the chance to train with the Premier League stars at Newcastle United.

Glenn Roeder was in charge, Michael Owen was in the squad, but was predictably injured and Kerr was given his chance.

Although he thought it was a cruel wind-up.

He said "I had been on trial at Stockport County in the week before, but then Ian Chandler rang and said Newcastle wanted me to spend time there.

"I thought he was taking the mick out of me.

"It was meant to be three days, but it turned into 11 days.

"I wasn't meant to be playing against Bolton, but I did, and then they had a friendly on the following week and they asked me to stay on.

"Wembley was a great experience; all three times were great experiences.

"But this was something completely different.

"Michael Owen was out injured, but I was training alongside Nobby Solano and Shay Given, big players in the Premier League.

"In the games I played up front with Albert Luque and Andy Carroll.

"So, there was me, a Northern League striker partnering a £10m player and a lad that would go on to be sold for £35m and play for England.

"I didn't drive at the time, so I was getting the Metro to training each day.

"I was walking in and you see all of the big-name players driving into the training ground in big, posh cars.

"It was all very different.

A deal could have been offered, but never materialised.

NORTHERN GOAL

Kerr went back to Whitley Bay and the Northern League.

One door had closed, but another opened and offered success beyond expectation.

Kerr explained "Glenn Roeder spoke to me and he said he would offer me a professional contract, but he didn't think I was ready for it.

"Nobody coming out of non-league would be ready for the Premier League to be honest.

"He said I would sit in the reserves and, when I think about it, as a Newcastle supporter, I should have done that

"But then what followed wouldn't have happened and it worked out well with the Wembley appearances."

Fast forward to the summer of 2011.

Glenn Roeder was long gone, Newcastle had been relegated, promoted and were yet to visit the new Wembley.

Kerr had been there, twice.

He was a two-time FA Vase winner with Whitley Bay and was still one of the Northern League's most-feared strikers.

His partnership with Paul Chow – dubbed 'Ker-Chow' by some – had fired the Seahorses to Wembley wins over Glossop North End and Wroxham.

Three would be a step too far surely? After all, Ian Chandler's side were now the big-hitters, they were the team to beat.

"We were a target for clubs, we know we were" admitted Kerr.

"I didn't expect us to do it twice in a row, so to even think about three times seemed crazy.

"We weren't the best team in the Northern League at the time and I think everyone knew that.

"But we had a togetherness, a spirit and a will to win games that got us through facing some very tough games.

"We never knew when we were beaten, so other clubs really targeting us didn't really bother us.

"We would always find a way to win."

By 2011, Whitley were a different side to the one that had won and retained the Vase in consecutive seasons.

They still had the silky skills of Paul Robinson, the classy Damon Robson and the evergreen goalkeeper Terry Burke.

But this side would have to work harder to win games, but they always tried to play on the front-foot.

THREE AND NOT SO EASY

"I think it was the way Chandler played his football," said Kerr.

"Throughout the whole time I played for him, he never changed.

"He had a system, he had a style of play and he stuck to it.

"Sometimes he would change, but it just always worked.

"He was like playing for Kevin Keegan, he just wanted to attack and playing in my position, I loved that.

"That was a big influence on the way the dressing-room was at the time.

"He loved to attack teams and go at them and that spread to every single player in the dressing-room.

"We were really ready to take anything on during the Vase and we were all pulling in the same direction."

The defence got underway with a narrow win at Thackley and a 7-1 hammering of AFC Liverpool at Hillheads.

That set up a long trip to Kent to face Herne Bay in the fourth round of the competition.

The holders were given a stiff test by their hosts but went ahead with a fine finish from Robinson.

Herne Bay equalised and looked set to become the side to put out the club that everyone wanted to beat.

But the team spirit kicked in, Chow got his chance and, inevitably, he took it to put his side through to a home tie against Dunstable Town.

"When you go that long without getting beat in any competition, other clubs are always going to raise their game against you.

"We just got past Thackley at their place, but then we had hammered AFC Liverpool at Hillheads.

"We went to Herne Bay and had a long trip down there.

"It was one of the toughest Vase games I have played in if I am honest with you.

"We felt as if they raised their game against us.

"We weren't at our best, in fact we were poor, but the togetherness kicked in and we got through.

"How we got through I don't know, but we did."

Dunstable were swept aside at Hillheads as Ker-Chow simply blew them away with two goals apiece in a 5-1 win.

That set up an all-Northern League quarter-final at Dunston UTS.

The tie would provide Kerr with solid proof that an unlikely treble of Vase wins was becoming a reality.

"Dunston UTS away was when I think we knew we could do it again.

"We didn't play as individuals and as a team.

"But when you have players like Paul Chow in your team, there is always a chance.

"He just needs one chance and if he gets it, he will take it.

"Dunston put us under serious pressure in that game and they will feel they should have beaten us.

"They would be right.

"I played with Chowy for six or seven seasons and he scored one goal outside of the area.

"That Dunston game typified him.

"He was there when we needed him, he did what he always does and scored vital goals."

An upwardly-mobile Poole Town provided the opposition in the last-four of the competition.

The away-leg was first up for Kerr and his team-mates, but their hosts had done their homework.

Chow was subjected to a physical battle, man-marked by two defenders and his influence on the game suffered.

But that created space for others and Damon Robson grabbed an equaliser before Kerr gave his side the upper-hand with a splendid free-kick.

"Poole was a tough trip," said Kerr.

"They were right up there as the favourites for the competition.

"We were getting beaten, again, and we weren't playing at the level we should have been.

"They did a job on Chowy, they man-marked him and they thought that getting him out of the game would give them a win.

"They had two tall centre-backs and they turned it into a battle.

"But we started getting more and more possession and grabbed two late goals.

"Damon Robson scored an equaliser and then I got a free-kick.

"There were a few lads that wanted to take it, but I got on it and fortunately it went in.

"I am sure I would have got some stick if it didn't."

THREE AND NOT SO EASY

Hillheads was rocking for the home leg of the semi-final.

Poole made the long trip North knowing that they had to go on the attack in order to overturn their first-leg deficit.

That gave Chow the space and time to do what he did best and Kerr revealed that he also answered a few critics in the away end that day.

"I remember their fans calling Chowy a donkey.

"That is my main memory of the game at Hillheads.

"Calling one of the best strikers at his level a donkey was only going to end one way really.

"He did what he does best and silenced them by helping us back to Wembley.

"The full-time whistle went, but it took a good few days to sink in that we had done it again.

"There had been changes to the squad, but the management team and the core of the squad were the same.

"We were friends, and it felt special to achieve what we did as a group."

The feared partnership of Chow and Kerr were both targeting a record at Wembley.

Both players could become the first to score in three consecutive finals in the same competition, not that Kerr was aware of that statistic.

He was more than happy to just focus on running out at the national stadium once again.

"I wasn't aware of the record.

"I was just happy to be playing at Wembley and I was solely focused on that.

"It was just nice to get on the score-sheet in the two previous finals.

"We kept everything the same in the build-up.

"We were in the same hotels and training was the same.

"It was just routine by then, it made it feel natural.

"Wembley felt like a place we wanted to be, and we felt at home then.

"It was still special, it was as special as the first year and it was as special as the second year.

"You couldn't change that, you couldn't change how it felt to walk out at Wembley."

Something was different this time around.

Whereas Glossop North End had been simple in 2009 and Wroxham had been a walk in the park 12 months later, this was different.

Coalville were a challenge, a real challenge, and one man kept Whitley in the game throughout.

Kerr said "We got information on Coalville Town and we got the usual stuff on them.

"We knew they were strong, but we didn't like adapting our game to match them.

"We just focused on ourselves and kept plugging away.

"But they were very good on the day.

"Terry Burke kept us in it, and he made some unbelievable saves and some great decisions.

"He was a top, top keeper and he marshalled us through some very tough moments in the final."

Despite the heavy pressure, Whitley went ahead with a goal from Chow just before the half-hour, but Coalville hit back with a goal from Matt Moore just after half-time.

Game on!

"Chowy got us ahead and it was a relief because we had been battered in the first 20 minutes.

"They kept the ball very well, but then we got a goal.

"They kept getting chances, we were riding our luck, but they just kept coming at us.

"They got back in it just after half-time and they could have gone ahead, but Terry kept them out."

Kerr's moment arrived just after the hour-mark.

Thirty minutes earlier, his partner-in-crime Chow had grabbed his customary Wembley goal.

Now it was Kerr's turn.

Robinson was the provider with a chop, not once but twice.

That created space for an inch-perfect cross that found the head of Kerr.

A glancing header took the ball into the far corner of the net and Whitley were edging towards yet another Vase win.

"If I am honest, I remember nothing of the goal.

"I have had to watch it back and I have done that many times.

"Steve Cuggy had told me to get across the front of the centre-back and make a nuisance of ourselves in there.

THREE AND NOT SO EASY

"I managed to do that, I got a little glance on the ball and thankfully it went in.

"But you don't think about the movement at the time, it just happens.

"It was just instinct, you just try to get in there and get something on it."

But Coalville kept coming.

The pressure was unrelenting.

The woodwork was hit, an inspired Burke made save after save, but an equaliser felt inevitable.

It duly arrived on 80 minutes as Adam Goodby was left unmarked in the area and headed past Burke from ten yards.

"They got another equaliser and I just felt as if it wasn't going to happen for us.

"A few lads were on their knees and it ended up being backs against the walls.

"Terry made more great saves, a few defenders managed to get some ridiculous blocks in and that kept us in the game.

"But, as I keep saying, we just never knew when we were beaten.

"We were all in this together, we knew we just needed one chance."

There was to be another goal and Whitley's deadly duo combined once again.

A Kerr free-kick found its way to Chow and the striker put his side ahead for the third time in the game.

In Kerr's own words "that was that".

He said "I took the free-kick and I had visions of the semi-final goal at Poole.

"I had a shot, I couldn't resist, and it went over the wall.

"They must have watched us because they had men on the line to block the free-kick.

"But that gave Chowy a chance and he stood in front of the keeper.

"It wasn't a great free-kick, but Chowy glanced it and their keeper parried it upwards.

"Then it's come down, hit Chowy on the calf and it went in.

"We knew that was it, we knew we had done it again, we knew it was our Vase now.

"They still had chances, but Terry kept them out and that was that."

The full-time whistle brought scenes of disbelief, relief and joy.

NORTHERN GOAL

This wasn't the classy display of the previous two seasons, this was something different.

This was grit, determination, never-say-die.

Kerr explained "It felt a bit different to the previous two years and it felt better to be honest.

"The Wroxham game was comfortable and at 6-1 it just wasn't a contest.

"You shouldn't beat any team by that score-line in a Wembley game.

"Even Glossop North End in the first year felt straightforward.

"But this was tough, this was a really difficult game.

"We shouldn't have won it really, we didn't deserve to win it, but the experience of being there before probably got us over the line.

"I had a drugs test after the game, and I was in there with two of their lads.

"They were gutted, and I understood why.

"The wins at Wembley bring so much joy, I don't tend to brag, and I don't rub it in people's faces.

"If people ask me then I talk about it, but they are memories I will never lose."

CHAPTER EIGHT

2012

HOMETOWN GLORY

FA Vase Final 2012

Dunston UTS 2-0 West Auckland

On the day of the Final

Prime Minister

David Cameron (Conservative)

Number One Single

Young (Tulisa)

At the Cinema

Battleship, The Dictator, Marvel's The Avengers

Football in 2012

Premier League Champions: Manchester City
FA Cup Winners: Chelsea
League Cup Winners: Liverpool
Champions League Winners: Chelsea
Europa League Winners: Atletico Madrid
Balon d'Or Winner: Lionel Messi (Barcelona)
PFA Player of the Year Winner: Robin Van Persie (Arsenal)
FA Trophy Winners: York City
Northern League Winners: Spennymoor Town
Northern League Division Two Winners: Team Northumbria
Northern League Cup Winners: Team Northumbria
Ernest Armstrong Cup Winners: Northallerton Town
Durham Challenge Cup Winners: Spennymoor Town
Northumberland Senior Cup Winners: Newcastle United Reserves

HOMETOWN GLORY

The sun shone brightly and cast long shadow across the hallowed turf of the UTS Stadium.

It's not even 9'clock in the morning, and there are still five hours to go until kick-off, but volunteers are swarming around performing all manner of tasks.

The place is always pristine for any game, but this is the FA Cup and National League North neighbours Gateshead are the visitors.

Even the BBC are on hand to capture the action, because this tie is one of the biggest in the history of Dunston UTS.

Temporary beer stalls are being filled, the programmes are being counted and the dressing-rooms are being given one last sweep by a familiar face.

He walks out of the away dressing-room, sweeping brush still in hand and a smile radiates from his face.

It is Billy Irwin, the man that led the club to their FA Vase Final win in 2012.

Despite leaving his role in the dugout two years prior, here he is, more than happy to describe himself as a "general dogsbody" at the club that is close to his heart.

But there is no time to stop, not even to admire the many images and mementoes that adorn the clubhouse walls baring Irwin's beaming face on that memorable Wembley day.

There are more tasks to do, the place must be ready.

This is commitment, this is passion, this is love.

This is his club, his home-town club.

Irwin said "I had played for the local school team and nothing came of trials at Darlington and Carlisle United.

"The Northern League had a youth league, it was called the Banks League.

"I joined Whickham and we were playing some top clubs like Spennymoor and Shildon, but we went and won the league.

"They only had a team for one year, but we won it.

"I went to North Shields and Colin Richardson was my manager.

"I played with people like Gary Nicholson and Ian Crumplin and we won the Northumberland Senior Cup beating Whitley Bay at St James Park.

"That was a good night, not that I can remember much about it.

"I wasn't playing too much, and I went to Durham City under Billy Cruddas.

"I stayed there for nine years, but I always thought I would end up at Dunston.

"I only lived just up the road, I always used to come here when Durham weren't playing.

"I knew everyone at the club, I loved the club and eventually Bobby Scaife brought me here.

"It was the right time to join and it was the start of a long relationship with the club.

"I love the club, I can't get enough of it."

Irwin's playing career was coming to an end and he was invited into the dugout as part of Scaife's coaching team.

The progression from player to coach, and then on to manager was made within the blink of an eye.

All of a sudden, the Dunston lad was the manager of his club.

He said "I was coming towards the end of my career and I couldn't get over them.

"Bobby asked me to help him in the dugout and Briggsy stepped up, so I became his assistant.

"I then stepped up as manager and it all seemed to happen so quickly.

"I didn't have time to take it in.

"You just start putting fires out and getting everything ready.

"It was such an honour to be manager of my club, to create memories with people I had known for years.

"I felt so proud.

"We did well in the Vase a few years running, but we had been beaten by the holders Whitley Bay here in a quarter-final in 2011.

"We thought it was our year, but Paul Chow scored and put us out.

"We learnt lessons that day."

With that Whitley Bay defeat still fresh in the mind, Dunston UTS kicked off their FA Vase campaign for the 2011/12 season with a home game against Blackwell Miners Welfare.

Irwin had watched their opponents, and even took his then-girlfriend (now his wife in case you are wondering) along on a scouting mission.

"We signed the likes of Chris Swailes and Steven Shaw during the following summer and we really fancied our chances," explained Irwin.

"Andrew Bulford hit the ground running that season and he was electric for us.

"We started in round two and hammered Blackwell at home.

"Bully got a hat-trick, Stephen Goddard did too, and we beat them 12-1, everything we hit went in.

"We had watched them down there, I went with my wife and she sat in the car with a packed-lunch whilst I watched the game.

"She knows the score, football and Dunston was my life.

"I wouldn't say she doesn't like football, but she won't watch it with me.

"She liked Wembley though."

Irwin had put together a team that was almost made for the Vase.

It was tough, it was hard-working and disciplined.

They had dangermen, but they just didn't know when they were beaten.

Results were ground out when they needed to be, everyone knew their roles in the side.

Everyone was willing to get in amongst the muck and the nettles to get a result.

Progress to the quarter-finals was accomplished with those qualities prominent.

Irwin explained "We didn't have luck, we didn't need it, we had a proper bloke's team.

"We made our own luck.

"We played Wisbech and we were getting beat because we had been dreadful.

"We were a goal down at half-time and I went mad at two players.

"We got them back to our place for a replay and beat them comfortably.

"In the next round Bethnal Green came up here.

"We watched them come off the bus and Harra said 'we've won this, they're f*****g freezing, look at them'.

"He was right, they didn't like the cold and we won it in the first-half.

"It was bitter, but they couldn't handle it.

"It just gave us even more proof that it was our year."

It wasn't a smooth passage to the last four of the competition.

A long journey to Peterborough North Star almost saw Dunston come unstuck.

Bulford, Ben Cattanach and Kane Young found the net in a seven-goal thriller that almost proved too much for Dunston's hard-working committee.

"The Peterborough North Star quarter-final was the sort of game you couldn't even make up," admitted Irwin.

NORTHERN GOAL

"We didn't play well, they had a big crowd and we were just poor.

"It went to extra-time, we were 2-1 down and then suddenly we were 3-2 up.

"They grabbed one back and then Bully scored late in extra-time.

"There were crazy scenes and some of the committee men had to walk away, they just couldn't believe it."

If that trip to Peterborough proved too much, then you have to wonder what a dramatic two-legged semi-final against Staveley Miners Welfare would do for anyone at the club.

A narrow lead was secured with a single-goal win in the home leg.

Predictably, Bulford was the match-winner.

But he would have an even more key role in the away leg, which went down in Dunston folklore for a whole host of reasons.

"The home leg was an awful game," said Irwin

"It was baking hot, the pitch was rock solid, it was a dour game.

"I nearly brought Bully off, but he turned and smacked one in, so we had a lead to hold on to in the away game.

"We were solid defensively, but we knew we had so much attacking strength too.

"Stephen Goddard was massive for us and he was quality.

"We knew 1-0 wasn't enough and there was still work to do.

"We couldn't go and play for a draw, we were tempted, but we knew we could score against them.

"We went a goal down, so it was level, but Bully got one back and got booked when the crowd pulled him over the fence.

"But then he made a rash challenge and got sent-off.

"I thought that was it, even more so when they scored and went in front ahead of half-time.

"They had a lad sent-off too because he elbowed Kane Young.

"Goddard scored a stunning goal to win it four minutes from the end of the game and that was it.

"What a day, it was maybe even a better feeling than Wembley."

Northern League title rivals West Auckland Town were to be Dunston's opponents at Wembley.

The two sides had forged a "competitive" rivalry over the past few seasons - something that only added to the big day for Irwin.

HOMETOWN GLORY

"Playing another Northern League side in the final didn't matter.

"There was a big rivalry between the two teams and clubs.

"It added to it and people still talk to me about it today.

"We played each other three or four times in that season and there was nothing in any games.

"They had so-called better players, we were the underdogs according to the bookies.

"We knew it would be a battle on the day, we were wary of everything about them.

"We knew how much they wanted to beat us, they just wanted to win any game, like anyone does."

Irwin and his players had another reason to want to secure the Vase.

Less than a year before the final, the club lost their much-loved physio and sports therapist Matty Annan.

He was a key part of their setup and someone that the players and coaches admired.

He was still with the squad on their trip to Wembley, albeit with a rather unique contribution to the dressing-room.

"We had been fortunate enough to have some brilliant volunteers and we had a great bloke called Matty Annan as our physio.

"We lost him sadly, but he went everywhere with his afterwards because we had some of his old underpants that we took with us.

"They had holes all over them, that doesn't even come close, but they were up in the changing-room where we went.

"Even Wembley."

In a remarkable turn of events, both Dunston UTS and West Auckland Town would head to Wembley on the back of Northern League title disappointment.

Supporters and officials from West were on hand to witness Irwin's side fall to a narrow defeat at Spennymoor Town in the penultimate game of the season, a result that handed the title to their hosts.

But there were no concerns about his side being ready for Wembley, despite their clear disappointment at missing out on topping the Northern League Division One table.

"The players were all friends and Chris Swailes always tells us all that we should have won the league that year.

"But the players put the disappointment of losing the league at Spennymoor behind them.

"I knew they were focused on Wembley and I could see that even more when we trained at Arsenal's academy.

"We had it for two hours and we couldn't get the players off the pitch.

"Arsenal were brilliant for us, they let us do whatever we wanted, and it was the perfect preparation for Wembley.

"The lads just loved it."

Wembley was a world away from the likes of Appleby Park and Old Ferens Park, where Irwin had plied his trade as a player.

His team selection was made, it was obvious in his own words.

But being pitchside at Wembley, where the likes of Sir Bobby Robson and Sir Alex Ferguson had showcased their managerial talents, had a different impact on Irwin.

It was just a game, just a pitch and a scoreboard.

He said "My mother could have picked our team, I think.

"Peter Dixon could have picked my team too and he knew what he was up against.

"It was boiling hot on the day, but I couldn't even sense that at pitchside.

"I was just focused on the game.

"If I am honest, I didn't even realise we were at Wembley sometimes.

"It was just a pitch and a scoreboard to me."

The opening-half of the game was competitive, and keenly contested.

Nerves were obvious, but this was Wembley and both North East pride and the Vase were up for grabs.

Despite not being at their best, Dunston took the lead through Bulford.

It was a goal that meant that the striker had scored in every round of the competition that season.

But it was probably his most important because he had calmed down his team-mates by edging them in front.

"It was a tough first-half and I had told the lads just to be themselves on the pitch," explained Irwin.

"Don't do anything differently because it's Wembley, just be ourselves.

"It was cagey and nervy, they shaded it if I am honest.

"But a long-ball from Liam Connell was flicked on by Goddard and that gave Bully a sight of goal.

HOMETOWN GLORY

"It was a brilliant finish, just flicked it over their keeper Mark Bell and it crept in.

"That calmed us down, because it had been tense."

Irwin was cool in the dressing-room, despite the baking hot temperatures in which he conducted one of the most important team-talks of his managerial career.

Keep calm was the focus, grab another goal, don't let them back into the game.

His players were "excellent" according to the man himself.

The Vase wouldn't slip from their grasp.

"I can't remember my half-time team-talk.

"It was roasting hot in the dressing-room, and I was trying to calm everyone down a bit.

"We were outstanding in the second-half.

"Matty Moffat had a goal disallowed for them, but we just kept going at them.

"Bully and Goddard hit the bar and I think we knew a goal was coming.

"Bully got another goal and it was a case of counting down the minutes from them.

"Chris Swailes was unbelievable, he was different class that day.

"He would have nutted his granny that day."

There were chances for West Auckland to play on Dunston's nerves, but Irwin's side could have been out of sight too.

Full-time arrived, Irwin's first thoughts were to speak to their men stood in the opposing technical area.

Once the gentlemanly customs were complete, he turned to his own coaches and the club's committee men, who were watching on from the stands with tears in their eyes.

The hard work, the long hours, it had all been worth it.

"I went straight to their assistant manager Paul Foster at full-time.

"I felt for him, I shook his hand and I knew how he would be feeling.

"They I embraced Harra.

"We had done it as a club, and we wanted to do it for the committee.

"To see their faces at full-time was one of the best moments of the day.

"There were tears, it just meant so much to us all."

NORTHERN GOAL

Dunston UTS had done it.

Less than 30 years after being formed as a works team under the name of Whickham Sports, just over 20 years since they joined the Northern League for the first time, they were Wembley winners.

A small village in Gateshead had triumphed on the biggest stage English football has to offer.

Irwin was overwhelmed.

"We might have been the club with the lowest population to have won the Vase.

"It's basically just two streets and the MetroCentre.

"The support was unbelievable.

"But everyone got behind us, everyone still has a story to tell from the weekend."

But perhaps there is no greater story than the hometown boy that helped deliver the Vase for the club he loved.

Whitley Bay celebrate the first of their four FA Vase Final wins at Hillheads in 2002 CREDIT JULIAN TYLEY

Whitley Bay celebrate the first of their four FA Vase Final wins in 2002 CREDIT JULIAN TYLEY

Whitley Bay FA Vase winners 2009 CREDIT JULIAN TYLEY

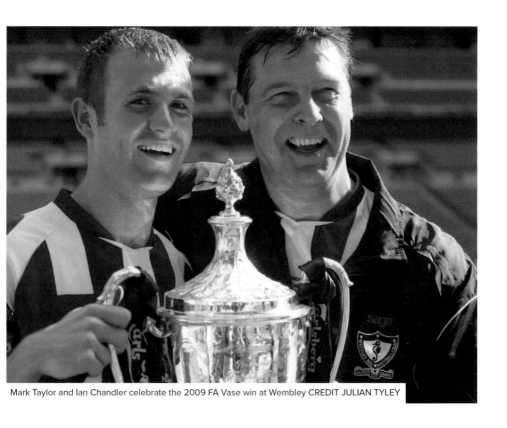

Mark Taylor and Ian Chandler celebrate the 2009 FA Vase win at Wembley CREDIT JULIAN TYLEY

Whitley Bay make it two in a row in 2010 CREDIT JULIAN TYLEY

Whitley Bay striker Paul Chow with his man of the match award for the FA Vase Final 2010 CREDIT JULIAN TYLEY

Lee Kerr is head over heels with delight after scoring for Whitley Bay in the 2011 Vase Final CREDIT JULIAN TYLEY

Three and easy for Whitley Bay as they secure a third consecutive Vase triumph in 2011 CREDIT JULIAN TYLEY

CHAPTER NINE

2013

FROM MILLA TO THE MOORS

FA Vase Final 2013

Spennymoor Town 2 Tunbridge Wells 1 (at Wembley Stadium)

On the day of the Final

Prime Minister

David Cameron (Conservative)

Number One Single

Get Lucky (Daft Punk featuring Pharrell Williams)

At the Cinema

The Great Gatsby, Fast and Furious 6, Star Trek Into Darkness

Football in 2013

Premier League Champions: Manchester United
FA Cup Winners: Wigan Athletic
League Cup Winners: Swansea City
Champions League Winners: Bayern Munich
Europa League Winners: Chelsea
Balon d'Or Winner: Cristiano Ronaldo (Real Madrid)
PFA Player of the Year Winner: Gareth Bale (Tottenham Hotspur)
FA Trophy Winners: Wrexham
Northern League Winners: Darlington
Northern League Division Two Winners: Crook Town
Northern League Cup Winners: Spennymoor Town
Ernest Armstrong Cup Winners: West Allotment Celtic
Durham Challenge Cup Winners: Bishop Auckland
Northumberland Senior Cup Winners: Ashington

FROM MILLA TO THE MOORS

Jason Ainsley has become part of the furniture at Spennymoor Town.

Over numerous spells with the club, in a whole host of different roles, he has become indelibly linked with everything at Brewery Field.

That included building the stands that surround the beloved home of the Moors.

A young Ainsley first joined Spenny at the age of 18 and was quickly put to work helping to build a new stand.

He is a man of many talents, one of them being his ability to build a team capable of success.

But building a stand, that was another matter.

"I joined when they were in the Northern Youth League," explained Ainsley.

"It was an under-19 league and I played really well against Spennymoor for Guisborough Town.

"They kept tapping me up and I just kept thinking about how far away it was from Stockton, where I lived.

"Then I took the leap and joined Spennymoor when Guisborough were trying to get me on a contract at the age of 18.

"I moved to Spennymoor on around £25 a week and I got a job.

"Ray Gowan was the manager and they were building a stand at Spennymoor.

"I can't put my name to building the stand because I couldn't put a trowel together.

"One of the other lads was helping build the stand, and my day consisted of playing penalty shoot-outs with a big Spenny fan called Nigel who used to come and watch the stand being built.

"I had one of the other lads watching for Ray Gowan and if he came, I would scarper up the stairs to get a bit muddy.

"I think I lasted four weeks and Ray said I don't think the job is for you."

Whilst Ainsley was struggling to do a job off the pitch, he had no such worries on it.

His form improved rapidly, and he quickly became a key part of the Moors line-up.

Football League clubs quickly took notice of the midfielder and one North East club decided to make their move.

"A lot of clubs were watching me, and I ended up joining Hartlepool United.

"I was probably a bit misguided because I had a lot of ability, but I didn't channel it in the right direction.

NORTHERN GOAL

"I went there and didn't do myself justice.

"I played something like 25 games and, although I did well in training, it was just missing me out in games.

"I then got a call from an agent that wanted to take me to Australia, and I thought why not, because my contract was up at the end of the season."

A move down under started a new chapter in Ainsley's life.

Although he struggled to settle in Australia, the young midfielder quickly adapted and became a key player for his club Inglewood.

There were temporary moves home with the likes of Blyth Spartans and, of course, Spennymoor.

There was even an unexpected meeting with a World Cup star that provided one of the most iconic celebrations in the tournament's illustrious history.

Ainsley said "I opened my suitcase when I first got to Australia and I had a load of good luck messages in there.

"I just burst out crying and I felt like getting on the first plane back home.

"I started to make friends and to settle in.

"I got player of the season in my first year, I played for the Western Australia team and we faced the likes of Nottingham Forest and West Ham United at the WACA, the big cricket ground over there.

"We went over to Indonesia and played a select team over there.

"They turned up and Roger Milla was in their side, I was in a bit of shock.

"I think he was about 50 by then, but he was still doing that bloody dance when he scored.

"The fans were absolutely fanatical, and they were throwing flares and all sorts.

"This was basically a pre-season game and it was like the final of the World Cup for them.

"I came home from that and got a call from the manager at the team in Australia saying he had a job in Singapore.

"The Asian football scene was really kicking off then with the J League in Japan and leagues in South Korea.

"I went over there and spent four years in the far-east, spending nine months over there, then coming home and playing for Spennymoor, Gateshead or Bishop Auckland.

"Then we decided to come home for family reasons."

Ainsley's move home naturally led him back to Spennymoor and he moved into coaching with the club that had found a place in his heart for so long.

FROM MILLA TO THE MOORS

Success was found as assistant manager to Jamie Pollock and Ainsley succeeded the former Middlesbrough and Manchester City midfielder in the main role in 2006.

A Northern League Division One title bid fell short and the club was in a mess off the pitch.

There was a serious threat to their long-term, but a new chairman gave the club new life and sent them on an upward trajectory.

Ainsley said "I took over as assistant manager and then Jamie Pollock took over as manager.

"We got promoted from the Northern League's second division and Jamie stepped down and I moved up to be manager.

"We had a lot of players from Middlesbrough like Craig Gott, Craig Ruddy and Andrew Peacock.

"They were top players, but it still haunts me that we didn't win that league.

"Financially, things weren't great, and we were working week-by-week.

"Benfield won the league, they scored in the last minute at Penrith and I threw my toys out of the pram blaming everyone but myself."

"The club was in dire straits and we wouldn't take potential new signings to the ground, because they wouldn't have signed.

"It was run down, the relationship with the council wasn't great.

"The chairman (Brad Groves) came in and everything changed.

"We felt immense pressure to deliver the Vase and we had become the big-hitters in the league.

"There was a jealousy and animosity towards us because we had won the league a few times and we were seen to be spending big money.

"But it was being done properly, with a structure in place at the club.

"It was going so well, but we wanted to win the FA Vase."

The Durham Challenge Cup, Northern League Cup and Northern League championship had all been delivered.

But the Vase stood out.

Ainsley watched on as league rivals Whitley Bay marched to Wembley and brought the Vase back to the North East, not once or twice, but thrice.

Dunston UTS were the next cab off the rank, and they etched their name on to the Vase with a 2-0 win in an all-Northern League final against West Auckland Town in 2012.

But when would it be Spennymoor's time in the sun? When would they meet the growing expectation that they would succeed at the home of English football?

Their latest bid to capture the Vase began with a severe test of their credentials at Bridlington Town in September 2012.

The Moors rose to the occasion and rarely slipped below those standards.

"We beat Bridlington Town away and it was one of the best performances I have ever seen from one of my sides," admitted Ainsley.

"It was 5-1 and everything was perfect.

"It all clicked, and they were a decent side by the way.

"Bridlington were a big name at the time, and I think word spread about what we had done.

"Then we became the team to fear.

"We hammered Benfield at home and got past Billingham Synthonia.

"I didn't like playing Northern League teams, it was a no-win situation for us."

All of a sudden, Ainsley and his side found themselves in round four of the competition.

Wembley wasn't on the horizon but talk that maybe this was their year had begun.

New names were plucked out of the hat but were vanquished by an increasingly confident Moors side.

"We started getting loads of home games against teams we had never heard of and we felt comfortable.

"We played Lordswood, Bemerton Heath and Gornal Athletic in the quarter-final and we didn't really know who they were.

"We got past them and then all of a sudden you are playing Guernsey in the semi-final."

That's right.

Guernsey!

An 880 mile round-trip was on the cards and that included a charted flight, an aborted landing, live television coverage and a first-leg on the Channel Island that was almost postponed.

"Guernsey! Who would have thought you would be playing a team like them in the FA Vase.

"We had to charter a flight to play them and I still say that was the best experience of the whole run.

"Going to the airport, seeing the supporters and seeing the flight signs.

"It was so surreal.

FROM MILLA TO THE MOORS

"Then we had to abort the landing because it was pouring down with rain.

"We got there eventually and then it was a long bus ride to the hotel.

"The next morning it was like there hadn't been any rain, it was a bright sunny day.

"There were queues a mile long at the ground and it was like a Football League game.

"I think there was about 4,000 there in green and white, so we took some stick.

"Then a helicopter came in and we didn't have a clue what was happening.

"They were trying to disperse the water on the pitch, which we didn't even realise was there, but the game was under serious threat.

"It was such a bizarre situation."

It was a bizarre situation, but the Moors made the best of it with a fine performance.

The dice were rolled, and they fell the way of Ainsley and his side.

Ainsley was forced into a regrettable early change as Wayne Phillips hobbled off with an injury.

But even that worked in his side's favour as Steven Richardson came on and made quite the impact.

"The game went ahead, despite the rain and the atmosphere was electric.

"Sometimes, in any cup run, there is a point when you think your name is on the cup.

"Wayne Phillips had started the game brilliantly, but he went off injured.

"We put Cogdon on the left and brought Steven Richardson on.

"It just worked, he scored, but they equalised.

"Then Speedy (Richardson) scored again in the second-half and Andrew Stephenson came on and made it 3-1 late on.

"We had a brilliant night, the chairman looked after us, but the flight back was a bit dicey and the landing was aborted at Newcastle again.

"We got home in the end, but it was a very surreal few days."

But there was still work to do in the second-leg at Brewery Field.

Guernsey made big noise ahead of the game, with manager Kevin Graham warning the Moors that they could pull off a surprise win in the North East.

A nervy 90 minutes saw the Brewery Field faithful put through the ringer.

They needn't have worried as their side flourished in front of the cameras once again.

Ainsley said "The big thing to take from the home leg was the fact that we had to kick off at 5 o'clock.

"Their local BBC station wanted to show the game and we couldn't break the Saturday live broadcasting laws.

"I can't even remember much about the game if I am honest, it was just a blur.

"I don't think it was a great game.

"Stephenson scored late on again and it was just a relief to get to Wembley.

"They were a good side.

"We were ready to face Shildon, we were sure we would be.

"But they got beaten by Tonbridge Wells, that was a shock."

The Moors were focused on Wembley.

Their Northern League campaign had ended with a runners-up spot, despite accumulating 109 points and losing only three of their 46 games during the season.

Darlington 1883 – just good old Darlington these days – had romped to the title with 122 points and a positive goal difference of 110.

But Ainsley's mind was on a difficult task ahead of their big day at the home of football.

Players, former colleagues and long-term friends were to be given the news they didn't want.

Ainsley was still relatively young for a manager, but he was about to be given one of the steepest learning-curves of his career.

"There were fantastic players in that side, and we were expected to win the final because we were so strong.

"I had to leave lads out of the final, not just the starting line-up, but the matchday squad.

"I was close with these lads, I had played with a lot of them, but I had to tell them that they weren't in the squad for Wembley.

"I left Craig Ruddy out of the squad, he was massive for us and Speedy (Richardson) was only on the bench, and he had scored in the semi-final.

"I think I'm a cuddly, friendly person, but that was one thing that I had to change.

"It was tough."

The big day arrived.

FROM MILLA TO THE MOORS

Naturally, it was baking hot, but isn't that just standard for any Wembley cup final?

Tunbridge Wells were the opposition after their shock semi-final win over Shildon.

Ainsley led out his squad, he represented his club, the club where he couldn't lay a brick all of those years ago.

The club he had kept coming back to and couldn't stay away from.

Pride doesn't even come close.

"I must have spent 30 years of my life at the club," he explained.

"Yes, I have been around other clubs, but to lead Spennymoor out at Wembley, a club I had captained, been a coach and managed, it was a feeling of immense pride.

"But there was a lot of anxiety and worry on the day, because we were heavy favourites.

"I didn't want to be the Northern League manager that didn't bring the Vase back.

"But we had big players and big characters that helped us manage with the expectation."

There may have been some nerves, but they didn't show.

The Moors got off to a flier and took the lead on 18 minutes with a header from Gavin Cogdon.

Influential midfielder Keith Graydon was the architect as his pinpoint cross dissected the Tunbridge defence, but Cogdon still had work to do.

The former Sunderland striker somehow arched his neck and buried a header beyond goalkeeper Chris Oladogba.

But the Moors couldn't add to their lead and the visitors found an equaliser 12 minutes from time when Josh Stanford took full advantage of an error of judgement by Robert Dean.

Ainsley was concerned.

"We got a goal through Cogdon, but we hadn't been great.

"We were comfortable, but we weren't at the level we could be.

"There was a massive crowd in there and maybe that put us on edge a bit.

"The second-half carried on that way, it wasn't a great spectacle.

"You couldn't see them scoring, and then Robert Dean has come for a ball and punched it.

"Deano is one of the best keepers at that level, but maybe he could have caught it.

"Their lad had flicked it over his head, and it was a great finish.

"That was on 78 minutes and you think maybe it's not going to be your day."

But this was to be the Moors day.

There was to be a winner and it came just four minutes after the equaliser.

Andrew Stephenson - a goalscorer in both legs of the semi-final — burst into the Tunbridge area.

He was surrounded by a number of defenders but twisted and turned before getting a shot away.

A desperate block sent the ball spiralling back to the penalty-spot.

Keith Graydon was alert and, without breaking stride, lashed a powerful shot into the ground and into the far corner of the net.

Pandemonium!

There were more chances, but the Moors held on.

Ainsley and his players had done it.

They had lived up to the expectations, they had delivered on the biggest stage of all.

"We reacted well to their goal, really well.

"Andrew Stephenson got into their area and they panicked.

"He somehow got a shot away and it got blocked, but it fell to Rasher (Keith Graydon) and he blasted it in.

"It was just draining, I was a wreck, but I was so proud.

"It was seeing the supporters at full-time, seeing the chairman's face and seeing everyone connected with the club getting what we all wanted.

"I saw people that had been through the whole journey with the club.

"We had brought some pride back to the club and to the town, which had seen a lot of depravation in the years prior to the final.

"It meant so much to us all.

"I went to bed that night and I was reading all of the congratulatory messages.

"I burst out crying, it was emotional."

The young lad not fit to lay bricks had taken his club to Wembley and brought pride and the FA Vase back to Spennymoor.

You could even forgive him for trying a Roger Milla dance after that journey.

CHAPTER TEN

2015

A PROMISE FULFILLED

FA Vase Final 2015

North Shields 2-1 Glossop North End (at Wembley Stadium)

On the day of the Final

Prime Minister

David Cameron (Conservative)

Number One Single

Cheerleader (OMI)

At the Cinema

Mad Max: Fury Road, Spy, Hot Pursuit

Football in 2015

Premier League Champions: Chelsea
FA Cup Winners: Arsenal
League Cup Winners: Chelsea
Champions League Winners: Barcelona
Europa League Winners: Sevilla
Balon D'Or Winner: Lionel Messi (Barcelona)
PFA Player of the Year: Eden Hazard (Chelsea)
FA Trophy Winners: North Ferriby United
Northern League Winners: Marske United
Northern League Division Two Winners: Seaham Red Star
Northern League Cup Winners: Shildon
Ernest Armstrong Cup Winners: Norton and Stockton Ancients
Durham Challenge Cup Winners: Shildon
Northumberland Senior Cup Winners: Blyth Spartans

A PROMISE FULFILLED

Football really is just a game.

For all the passion, anger, frustration and happiness that it provides, it really is just a group of men, women or children kicking a ball around a patch of grass.

But sometimes it can become more than just a game.

Sometimes it can help people cope and manage a tough situation in their life.

Gareth Bainbridge knows that all too well.

The striker has become a legend in the famous red of the Robins of North Shields and there is an almost unique relationship between the player and the club.

A bond has been forged, nurtured and strengthened throughout a period of Bainbridge's life where emotions were polarised to an extent rarely seen.

He helped deliver an unlikely FA Vase win for the club, all against a backdrop of losing his father Brian in heart-breaking circumstances.

North Shields as a club, his team-mates, supporters and the coaching-staff helped him deliver on a promise in a grand manner.

The bond started to grow within weeks of Bainbridge's move from Ashington in the summer of 2013.

He said "I was on a bit of a decline at Ashington and for the last two seasons I wasn't enjoying my football.

"I didn't realise that at the time.

"A few offers came in and I thought it was going to be hard to leave.

"I had been there for a few years, I had a lot of friends at the club and North Shields were only a Second Division team at the time.

"But I just wanted to get back to enjoying football once again.

"I spoke to (manager) Graham Fenton and (assistant manager) Andy Bowman and I liked them both.

"Then I discussed it with Ben Richardson, who I knew from school.

"He said it would be the best coaching I would get, and I knew it was for me.

"I never expected it to be the success that it was, I just wanted to play football on a regular basis and rediscover my passion for the game."

Bainbridge and his new club hit the ground running and the striker quickly became one of the most-feared players in the Northern League's second-tier.

Promotion was secured within 12 months of his arrival and it was achieved with relative ease.

NORTHERN GOAL

The Robins scored over 140 goals and ended the season with a century of points as their talented young squad reacted to the methods imposed on them by former Aston Villa and Blackburn Rovers star Fenton.

Bainbridge was flourishing, he had found a home and rekindled his love of the game.

"I had a full pre-season, I had stayed fit and I really focused on my fitness.

"I got my confidence back and I was scoring goals.

"It felt natural, I wasn't even thinking about scoring goals, it was just happening for me.

"Any striker will tell you that you will always gain confidence when the momentum is building, and the chances are coming your way.

"That happened in that first season at North Shields and within a year I felt as if I had found a home."

The connection between supporters, players and coaching-staff was almost unbreakable.

There was a trust between the three parties that strengthened the club as they prepared for a tilt at the leading lights in the Northern League.

Trust was at the centre of their relationship and Bainbridge believes that they became a force to be reckoned with because the club were so united.

"It is hard to describe the feeling in the dressing-room during that summer.

"We trusted Graham Fenton so much, we didn't doubt him, and we knew that he would bring in players that would help us.

"We knew that the players he signed would fit into the way we played, but they would also fit into the squad as a group of lads.

"The personality was key with every signing and we had a group of good lads that trusted each other and, more importantly, trusted the manager and his coaches.

"The supporters bought into it all.

"They are nuts, in a good way.

"We were getting 300 or 500 to league games and that was so different to other clubs in the league.

"It drove you on, you were in a game thinking if they showed that much passion then I have to as well."

The new season approached rapidly, new signings were made, final preparations were well underway.

A target-setting session was carried out and a light-hearted comment by a team-mate suddenly became a focus for the season.

A PROMISE FULFILLED

"We had a session where we set targets for all of the competitions.

"One of the competitions was the Vase and somebody in the squad said we should target the quarter-final.

"We all laughed at that.

"I think it was James Luccock said how about the semi-final?

"Everybody laughed, but nobody was laughing when Fenton told us we had set our target with that comment."

Their Vase run got underway with a narrow win at Northern League Division Two club Northallerton Town.

A 1-0 win was secured thanks to a goal from Dan Smart – who only managed to play in the game because he was working in North Yorkshire on the day of the game.

His job? He helped lay new surfaces on major roads.

A Highways Operative had put the Robins on their own road that would lead to Wembley.

Fellow Northern League clubs Stokesley, Sunderland RCA, Seaham Red Star and Consett were all sent packing, but it was the game against the latter that made Bainbridge and his team-mates find a role that they could relish.

"We played a lot of Northern League teams and I think that worked in our favour.

"But what also worked in our favour was the fact that we were newly-promoted.

"A lot of opposition sides dismissed us.

"I remember playing Consett and we were four goals up.

"Their centre-back grabbed hold of me and he was asking me how we were beating them so easily.

"That showed a total disrespect to us and it showed what we could do throughout the competition.

"We were always underdogs, but we loved that."

The Vase run was getting serious now.

The 4-1 home win against Consett set up a fifth round tie against high-flying Southern Counties East club Phoenix Sports.

The visitors were unbeaten in the league ahead of their visit to North Tyneside and were seen as one of the favourites to lift the Vase that season.

In front of a four-figure crowd, Bainbridge scored twice in a 4-1 win as the Robins made a mockery of the pre-match predictions from the "experts".

NORTHERN GOAL

Wembley was quickly becoming prominent in his mind.

"We played Phoenix Sports in the round before the quarter-finals.

"They came up to our place, they were unbeaten in their league, and all of the talk was about how it would be a step too far for us.

"They were touted as a big team and there were also clubs like Shaw Lane that were a potential favourite too.

"Those clubs started getting knocked out of the competition and all of a sudden there was talk about the luck of the draw falling our way.

"We beat Phoenix quite comfortably and that was when I started talking to my family about getting to Wembley."

Bainbridge was flying, everything was going his way.

Goals were expected every time he pulled on a North Shields shirt and he delivered them with aplomb.

But away from football a serious situation was developing.

Bainbridge's Dad Brian was taken into hospital with a "minor illness".

Time passed, but a recovery still seemed at arm's length.

A lift was needed, but both images of his son's goalscoring exploits and talk of Wembley failed to provoke the reaction that was desired.

Bainbridge explained "Dad had a head injury around 12 years ago and he lived in a care home.

"He used to come to a few of my games, but things were difficult in that sense.

"When we played in the Northumberland Senior Cup, I would never tell him until we reached the final.

"It was different with this run and that's why the Phoenix Sports game stands out for me.

"He went into hospital with a minor illness, it was cellulitis.

"I had a couple of photos from the Phoenix game and I thought I would show him them to try and pick him up a bit because he was very low.

"It was to give him a reason to keep strong and I told him we were a couple of games from Wembley.

"He was so emotional about my football, but there was no reaction to them.

"Looking back, I think he knew he wasn't going to be at Wembley.

There were no signs of an improvement.

Multiple organ failure led to his passing three days after he was taken to Gateshead's Queen Elizabeth Hospital.

A PROMISE FULFILLED

Bainbridge had delivered a promise to his Dad in the hours before they met for the final time

"He went in on the Tuesday and passed away on the Friday.

"I visited him on the Friday, and I was there with him all day and all night.

"I made a promise to him on that day that I would score at Wembley, but I think that he would just have wanted me to enjoy the day and enjoy the game.

"He was my best mate.

"My Mam and sister told me I had to go home and get some rest.

"I did, and that was when he passed away with multiple organ failure, which came from an infection in his body that was linked to the cellulitis."

Football was suddenly secondary, but friendship and respect were always there.

Bainbridge has never hidden from the fact that he admired a number of key figures at North Shields and what happened next is a key reason why he holds so much affection for them.

"Dad's funeral was two days before the Vase quarter-final against Erith and Belvedere.

"The likes of Fenton, Andy Bowman and Ben Richardson came to the funeral, but they didn't tell me they were coming.

"Fenton caught up with me after the funeral and told me to have a couple of days to just relax and enjoy myself.

"Then he started me on the Saturday, and I remember thinking that I hoped he wouldn't treat me any differently.

"I think there were about five minutes on the clock, and he screamed at me for not reacting to a ball in their area.

"It was the best thing he could have done for me.

"Football helped me through it all.

"Fents had a long chat with me and he knew what I was going through because he lost his Dad at a young age.

"But because of the run, when I look back now, I realise just how much it took my mind off losing my Dad.

"I knew I didn't have to go through everything on my own."

A two-legged semi-final tie saw North Shields make the long trip to Wiltshire to face Hellenic League title challengers Highworth Town.

A 1-0 was secured by a Dean Holmes goal in front of a boisterous band of travelling support.

NORTHERN GOAL

But the performance of one team-mate left an injured Bainbridge fearing for his place in the starting line-up for the home leg of the tie.

"I was injured for the first-leg and I tweaked a hamstring at Penrith a few days earlier," explained the striker.

"I trained at Villa Park on the way down and I felt alright.

"But Fenton kept saying that it was all about the tie being over two legs.

"Dean Walker played, and he was absolutely brilliant.

"The fans were unbelievable down there and we won 1-0 with a goal from Dean Holmes.

"I didn't think I would play in the second-leg if I am honest."

He shouldn't have worried.

Bainbridge was restored to the starting line-up for the second-leg and predictably he made an impact on the game.

It was his second-half goal that settled any nerves amongst the Robins faithful and a place at Wembley was secured by a late Holmes goal.

Bainbridge had been replaced by the time the full-time whistle had been blown but rushed to spend time with his family.

In his words "All of the talk was about how I was coping with Dad's loss, how the club and supporters had helped me through it.

"But they had been through it too, and all I wanted was to spend time celebrating reaching Wembley with them."

After all of the talk, the media interest, the routine visit to the national stadium and the completion of the league season, it was time for the big day.

The Robins were seen as the outsiders for the final against North West Counties League champions Glossop North End.

Nerves were only natural, but not clear for Bainbridge on the morning of the game.

"I don't think I realised how nervous I was in the hotel," he admitted.

"I shared a room with Ben Richardson, and he was telling me to calm down.

"I was on Twitter looking at news articles about myself and the team, I was on edge to be honest.

"I just wanted to enjoy it, but because of the hype I thought I wouldn't.

"Fenton told me to just enjoy it and settle down.

"But daft things like Adam Forster doing block tackles in Fenton's room as a fitness test and Dean Holmes doing sprints in the car park.

A PROMISE FULFILLED

"That settled us down."

Those nerves were further soothed by a controlled, measured team-talk from Fenton and his coaching-staff.

There was no time for hyperbolic hysteria, this was calmness personified.

The two sides tussled for superiority during an underwhelming first-half.

The Robins more than matched their much-fancied opponents, but the game was goalless at the interval.

But that all changed within ten minutes of the restart as Tom Bailey made the most of some poor defending from North Shields to put North End ahead.

Bainbridge, so often a hero at the other end of the pitch, had become a villain by switching off in his own area.

He revealed "It was my man.

"I completely switched off.

"I thought the referee was going to give a penalty and then I thought the ball was going out of play.

"But it's come back into the area and I am walking back to the halfway line along with James Luccock and Jack Donnison.

"They had three men at the far-post and my player scored.

"All I could think about was what Fenton was going to say.

"I was devastated."

Time ticked on.

The dream was slipping away.

Sixty minutes, seventy minutes, eighty minutes passed without an equaliser.

But then, from a corner-kick, Bainbridge's moment arrived.

His opportunity to deliver on a promise presented itself.

Naturally, it was taken.

"We had a corner routine and it worked throughout the season.

"Kevin Hughes would make a dummy run to the near post and scream at the corner taker asking why they hadn't played it.

"I would make my run and Kev would block my marker.

"The problem was I was exhausted, and I was walking to the edge of the area by the time Kev has started his move.

"I was late, and I was miles away from where I should be.

"My concern was that Fenton would go mad.

99

NORTHERN GOAL

"But Michael McKeown stuttered his run and it gave me time to get to where I should be.

"The keeper missed it and I got on the end of it.

"Time stood still, the ball went into the net and I ended up clung on to the post."

Suddenly, this natural goalscorer was thrust into a very unnatural situation for a non-league player.

He had scored on the biggest stage English football has to offer.

He had delivered on the promise he made to his Dad in the dark hours before his passing.

Relief, exaltation and joy overcame Bainbridge.

His usual knee-slide celebration followed, but it was twinned with a moment of remembrance.

A moment between father and son, a moment of shared joy and pride.

"It was relief when I scored, that was the only emotion I can remember.

"It went silent for three or four seconds.

"Then I heard something, and I wanted to do the knee-slide, that was always on my mind.

"I thought the pointing skywards was something done for the benefit of others.

"But I felt like I would be leaving Dad out if I didn't do that.

"It was for him and it was for me.

"As soon as the celebration was done, I felt a relief and I heard my name on the scoreboard.

"Then it was back into game-mode."

Ah yes, the game was still there to be won.

The winner would duly arrive in the fifth minute of the first period of extra-time.

Adam Forster got it, but it could and should have been Bainbridge.

The moment, the missed opportunity, the what could have been still rankles with a man that feeds on goals.

"Denver Morris was unbelievable that day and he won us the game as much as anyone else.

"I was still on the pitch when he set the winner up and I am still gutted about it.

A PROMISE FULFILLED

"I knew the movements to make to get on any cross.

"I timed my run perfectly and Denver's cross was superb.

"But it went under my foot and I was devastated.

"Fozzy came in back-post and put it in with a brilliant finish.

"It was a great moment, but I was still gutted that I didn't get the second."

North End went increasingly direct in their desperate search for an equaliser.

Long ball after long ball peppered the Robins back-line, but they were repelled by a sturdy defensive partnership of Kevin Hughes and John Parker.

One last desperate hack clear came from Kieran Wrightson and it was met by the joyous noise of the full-time whistle.

The Robins had done it, they were the Northern League's latest FA Vase winner.

Bainbridge was immediately overwhelmed with emotion.

"I was bubbling at full-time and I was saying to Brian Smith to look at everything.

"The scoreboard, the fans, everything.

"I ran on to be with the lads and all I could say was we have won the Vase, we have won the Vase, we have won the Vase.

"We went to get the cup and I did everything I could do to get into the photos as he lifted it.

"I pushed my way in, I made sure I was near him.

"I wanted that moment."

It was a moment, a day and an achievement that Bainbridge and his family had earned.

Andrew Bulford wheels away in celebration after putting
Dunston UTS ahead in the 2012 final CREDIT KEN FITZPATRICK

Dunston UTS manager Billy Irwin celebrates their 2012 FA Vase Final win CREDIT KEN FITZPATRICK

Moors the merrier as Ainsley's men celebrate their 2013 FA Vase Final win CREDIT DAVID NELSON

A happy homecoming for the Moors in 2013 CREDIT DAVID NELSON

Goalscorers Gareth Bainbridge and Adam Forster celebrate North Shields 2015 FA Vase Final win CREDIT IAN WARDE

Manager Graham Fenton sprays champagne over the North Shields players and coaching staff after their 2015 FA Vase Final win CREDIT IAN WARDE

Morpeth Town management team Nicky Gray and Dave Malone celebrate with the FA Vase CREDIT ANDY NUNN

Julio Arca in action during the 2017 FA Vase Final CREDIT KEVIN WILSON

Chris Swailes is mobbed by his Morpeth Town team-mates after scoring the equaliser in the 2016 Vase Final CREDIT ANDY NUNN

CHAPTER ELEVEN

2016

PLAYING WITH HEART

FA Vase Final 2016

Morpeth Town 4-1 Hereford FC

On the day of the Final

Prime Minister

David Cameron (Conservative)

Number One Single

One Dance (Drake featuring Wizkid and Kyla)

At the Cinema

X-Men: Apocalypse, The Nice Guys, The Angry Birds Movie

Football in 2016

Premier League Champions: Leicester City
FA Cup Winners: Manchester United
League Cup Winners: Manchester City
Champions League Winners: Real Madrid
Europa League Winners: Sevilla
Balon d'Or Winner: Cristiano Ronaldo (Real Madrid)
PFA Player of the Year Winner: Riyad Mahrez (Leicester City)
FA Trophy Winners: FC Halifax Town
Northern League Winners: Shildon
Northern League Division Two Winners: South Shields
Northern League Cup Winners: Shildon
Ernest Armstrong Cup Winners: Northallerton Town
Durham Challenge Cup Winners: Newton Aycliffe
Northumberland Senior Cup Winners: North Shields

PLAYING WITH HEART

It was the sort of news that sends shockwaves through your body and a shiver down the spine.

Words are being spoken, but barely make sense.

The world pauses for just a second, then carries on around you as you process a life-changing piece of news.

A career spanning three decades and 16 clubs was under serious threat.

Dunston UTS defender Chris Swailes had played for the likes of Bury and Rotherham United in the Football League, but now his career was close to being ended by an atrial fibrillation.

The problem came to a head in a game at Dean Street, home of Dunston's Northern League rivals Shildon.

Swailes explained "I came off at Shildon and I knew there was something wrong with me.

"I couldn't walk up the stairs, I couldn't chew chewing gum, I couldn't even brush my teeth in the build-up to the game.

"I told Billy (Irwin, Dunston UTS manager), but I said I could play.

"Within five minutes I was off the pitch.

"I went to run for a ball, and I couldn't breathe, I couldn't move, I went down to my knees on the pitch.

"I managed to get my breath eventually, but I went straight to hospital.

"My heart had gone out of rhythm and when that happens, it becomes very serious.

"I had loads of tests, had three cardio versions at different times and then had oblation surgery on my heart.

"They cut two ventricles out to make it easier for the blood flow around my heart.

"I was told that it was a fit heart when I was operated on, so it was a shock."

Just months after helping Dunston UTS win the FA Vase, Swailes faced the prospect of giving up a career in the game that he loved so dearly.

The big defender underwent keyhole surgery to resolve the issue, but even then, an issue arose that would complicate his recovery.

Resuming his playing career seemed further away than ever before.

"When I had the oblation surgery, the surgeon nicked the phrenic nerve, which controls your breathing.

"Therefore, I could do nothing for six months to a year.

"I couldn't do anything, and I was on beta blockers and warfarin.

NORTHERN GOAL

"I had to bide my time, ease myself in gently and just take things slowly.

"I started jogging and slowly started to get back to normal.

"I didn't think I would get back playing, so I took a coaching job in Scotland with Hamilton Academcials.

"I didn't think I would get my boots back on as a player, so that felt like the next move for me.

"It didn't work out, but that offered me a new opportunity."

It was a work colleague that offered Swailes a new start and put him on the path to writing his name in the Wembley history books.

He said "I knew Nicky Gray at Morpeth Town from working at Gateshead College.

"He offered me a chance to join them as cover for their centre-back options.

"I was comfortable with that role and I didn't think I would be anywhere near first-choice.

"David Hiftle was doing really well, and I played one in every five or six games.

"I felt comfortable, I was doing well, I felt at ease in the game once again.

"My fitness was being managed by Nicky and myself and, if I felt tired, I was rested.

"David (Hiftle) got a bad injury, Chris Reid was cup-tied when he joined from Whitley Bay.

"It ended up being Michael Hall and myself as the centre-back partnership throughout the Vase run.

"It was like the parting of the red sea.

"Things just opened up and fell my way."

It was far from plain-sailing in the Vase for the Highwaymen.

The Craik Park club safely negotiated qualifying round ties at Padiham and Billingham Synthonia to progress into the first round.

A trip to the North West was their prize and a visit to Hallmark Security League club West Didsbury and Chorlton, but their road to Wembley almost ended as soon as it began in a remarkable fixture.

Morpeth eased their way to a commanding lead as goals from Michael Chilton, James Novak, Jordan Fry and Swailes himself handed their side a four-goal advantage at the interval.

The tie took place on 31st October and the Highwaymen produced a Halloween horror show in the second-half as their hosts roared back into the game.

PLAYING WITH HEART

Two goals from Matty Kay and one apiece from Ash Woods and Nic Evangelinos had Swailes and his team-mates rocking.

The exit was drawing ever closer, only to be narrowly avoided by a last-gasp goal.

"We should have gone out at West Didsbury and Chorlton," admitted Swailes.

"We were four up at half-time and it should have been ten.

"They came back to 4-4 and we were dead on our feet.

"They should have gone ahead and had a couple of very good chances to go through and put us out.

"But then Michael Chilton, in the last seconds of the game, scored with a header and that was the most remarkable moment of the run for me.

"I thought we were gone, I thought we were done, but somehow we went through to the next round.

"It wasn't the only time it happened, maybe we were just fated to be in the final."

It wasn't the only narrow escape that Morpeth pulled off during their run.

They were controversially handed a walkover by the Football Association after 1874 Northwich revealed that they couldn't find a squad to travel to the North East for a hastily-rearranged fixture.

It was harsh to say the least.

A titanic tie against South Shields saw the two sides go head-to-head on a freezing cold night in Consett.

Six goals were evenly shared, and an equally epic penalty shoot-out took place as the Highwaymen finally prevailed with a 10-9 win from the spot.

More lucky escapes came with a fourth round tie against Northern League rivals North Shields and a semi-final first-leg against Essex-based Bowers and Pitsea.

Swailes takes over.

"We were down to ten men at North Shields and they were holders of the Vase at the time.

"Our goalkeeper Karl Dryden saved a penalty.

"Well, I say saved a penalty, it actually hit him in the face.

"Sean Taylor got two goals and we sneaked through there too.

"We had a great escape in the semi-final away leg.

"We went to Bowers and Pitsea and we were two ahead, but we conceded from set-pieces.

"We couldn't believe how good we had been in the first-half, but here we were on the rack and they were all over us.

"We went into our shells but got out of there with a draw.

"I think it's moments like that when you believe your name is on the Vase.

"The home game proved it.

"We didn't believe anyone could come to Craik Park and beat us.

"It was a fortress, we knew that, we knew how strong we were at home."

Morpeth had escaped from their trip to Essex with a 2-2 draw and Swailes' confidence in their ability on their own patch was well-placed.

Sean Taylor handed his side a perfect start as he fired them in front after just four minutes, but the visitors got back on level-terms with a goal from Lewis Manor just moments before half-time.

Nerves were frayed, but the Highwaymen always looked in control.

Their cause was helped when Bowers and Pitsea were reduced to ten men with 10 minutes remaining as Ross Adams received a second yellow card for pulling back Town midfielder and former FA Vase winner Keith Graydon.

That handed the initiative to Morpeth and a late volley from Luke Carr confirmed their Wembley date and set off wild celebrations inside Craik Park.

But for Swailes, the immediate reaction was to worry about his ability to stay fit for the final.

"They (Bowers and Pitsea) didn't have a lot of quality, but they worked hard and pressed us.

"Our quality shone through, but it was a hard-fought game on a bog of a pitch.

"We got through and my biggest fear suddenly hit me.

"I was tense about getting an injury and I was visiting a chiropractor every week to get my back cracked.

"You're still young in the mind, but you know you have to look after yourself.

"I played two or three games between the semi-final second-leg and Wembley.

"I just had to hold on and make sure I was ready, but the lads helped me too.

"We had a strong dressing-room and we had goals all over the place.

"We supported each other, we had that spirit, so we knew we could trouble everyone in the competition and that included Hereford."

PLAYING WITH HEART

Ah yes – Hereford.

The all-conquering phoenix club of Hereford United.

The Bulls had enjoyed a prosperous first season in existence and were looking to complete a remarkable quadruple after winning the Midland League Premier Division, Herefordshire County Cup and the Midland Football League Cup.

A Wembley win was almost inevitable according to most experts and Swailes believes that the Bulls manager and one-time Football League opponent Peter Beadle shared that opinion.

"We visited Wembley two or three weeks before the final.

"There was Nicky, me and a few others and we met their manager.

"We were shown around the stadium, in the dressing-rooms, in the boxes and went pitchside.

"We sensed a confidence from him, we knew it was over-confidence and that would work against him.

"I remember playing against Peter Beadle in the Championship when he was at Port Vale and I was at Bury.

"Keith Graydon mentioned that they had not been to watch us and that said it all."

Hereford were massive favourites going into the Vase final and almost monopolised the media focus ahead of the game.

They were also backed by over 20,000 supporters at Wembley and paraded 'Ronaldo' ahead of the game.

Morpeth were the red rag and the Bulls were ready to charge.

Swailes admitted that it was all a distraction and his nerves weren't helped by the fact that his side fell behind inside three minutes to a goal from Rob Purdie.

"They had a massive support at Wembley.

"That distracted us, and I don't mind admitting I was nervous.

"I have played over 1,200 games in my career and I have only been nervous in two games.

"That was Dunston in the Vase final and this game – but I knew it was because I shouldn't be there, not at my age.

"They scored early, and a lot of things go through your head.

"You worry that it is going to go the way that many people were saying.

"They were all over us and Karl Dryden made a couple of massive saves to keep it down to one.

NORTHERN GOAL

"We had to stay tight, stay compact and just ride it out.

"They were flying, and we just had to stick together as a team."

Highwaymen keeper Karl Dryden put in an inspired performance as his goal was put under serious pressure.

One save to deny livewire winger Sirdic Grant seemed to inspire his side, who slowly got to grips with the game as the half-hour approached.

"It was wave after wave of attack, but we knew we would break out.

"It was heading towards half-time and we were still in the game.

"We had grown into it, we had kept the ball, we were improving and getting more confident.

"We started causing them problems and we just needed a goal.

"I think they eased off because they thought it was game over.

"Their over-confidence was working against them."

On 34 minutes, Swailes' big moment arrived.

Sean Taylor drove into the Bulls area and forced a corner that allowed the centre-back to make a rare venture outside of his own half.

As Ben Sayer made his way to take the corner-kick, Swailes took up a different position to his usual stance of "impacting the goalkeeper".

It was a move that would see him write his name into Wembley history.

Bulls goalkeeper Martin Horsall misjudged Sayer's cross and that allowed Swailes to force the ball over the line in any way he could.

Pandemonium ensued.

Just two years after his heart operation, 45-year-old Swailes became Wembley oldest cup final goalscorer.

Coincidentally, the goal also came 23 years after he had made his Football League debut for Doncaster Rovers against Hereford United.

Swailes said "I was always the one that impacted the goalkeeper.

"Because of my age, I'd use anything to do that.

"A knee, an elbow, standing on his foot, just anything!

"But I went back-post and it was a case of see what happens.

"I saw the ball sail over the keeper's head and I just thought that I had to get something on the ball.

"It hit my midriff and bobbled over the line.

"It was the best way of finishing, that's what I tell people anyway.

PLAYING WITH HEART

"I thought the heart problems were going to finish my career.

"But, to say I would score in a Vase final, never mind even play again, was remarkable.

"It is unbelievable, and I don't tend to look back at achievements.

"But that is one that I am very proud to have in my career."

The Bulls were rocking as half-time approached.

This wasn't in the plan, this wasn't how it was meant to be.

The team that nobody was talking about were suddenly taking control.

"They had given us their best shot and they only had one goal," said Swailes.

"If they got a second goal, I think they would have gone on to win it.

"But we were level and we were confident.

"The dressing-room was buzzing, and we knew we could do it.

"Wembley is a mental and physical battle and we had the will to win both of those battles.

"If we raised it as we knew we could, we would win the Vase."

To put it simply, Morpeth were outstanding in the second-half.

They absorbed pressure, they picked their passes, they were strong, they were quick, and Hereford had no answer to what they were facing.

Luke Carr put Morpeth ahead within 40 seconds of the second-half getting underway.

He dabbed in celebration, but nobody complained.

Sean Taylor extended the lead before the hour-mark with a neat finish after a delightful pass from Chilton.

The cherry on the cake came in injury-time as substitute Shaun Bell added a fourth goal less than two minutes after replacing Carr.

The final whistle came, Swailes was a three-time FA Vase winner.

"Every player did what was asked of them.

"We did that so well and we saw it through comfortably in the end.

"The whistle went, and I can remember every second of that moment.

"I don't get emotional, I am a professional and it was a case of it was job done for me.

"That's not to say I didn't enjoy it, or revel in it, but it was more a case of taking everything in.

NORTHERN GOAL

"Seeing my children, my wife and the supporters, I just wanted to take everything in and enjoy it all.

"It was just a perfect day."

The career that was almost ended by heart problems had been given a silver lining.

Swailes was a history-maker.

"It was a swan-song, I was lucky, it was a lucky six months and I capped it off at Wembley.

"I left home at 16 and didn't come back to the region until I was 38.

"It was a love of the game that kept me going and the drive, the competition, trying to better yourself and get the better of lads that are half your age.

"If I wasn't in football, I would be doing something in fitness.

"But I am proud to have been involved in the game and moments like that final, scoring at Wembley, winning the Vase with a great group of lads, that all makes it worth the stress and the effort."

CHAPTER TWELVE

2017

PREMIER CLASS

FA Vase Final 2017

South Shields 4-0 Cleethorpes Town

On the day of the Final

Prime Minister

Theresa May (Conservative)

Number One Single

Despacito (Luis Fonsi and Dandy Yankee featuring Justin Bieber)

At the Cinema

Alien: Covenant, Baywatch, Wonder Woman

Football in 2017

Premier League Champions: Chelsea
FA Cup Winners: Arsenal
League Cup Winners: Manchester United
Champions League Winners: Real Madrid
Europa League Winners: Manchester United
Balon d'Or Winner: Cristiano Ronaldo (Real Madrid)
PFA Player of the Year Winner: N'Golo Kante (Chelsea)
FA Trophy Winners: York City
Northern League Winners: South Shields
Northern League Division Two Winners: Stockton Town
Northern League Cup Winners: South Shields
Ernest Armstrong Cup Winners: Northallerton Town
Durham Challenge Cup Winners: South Shields
Northumberland Senior Cup Winners: Blyth Spartans

PREMIER CLASS

This was a world away from Wembley.

The grass was long, uneven and unforgiving.

Players crunched into tackles, with the threat of ice-cold water and the magic sponge never too far away.

The play was hurried, reckless and careless.

Passes went astray, crosses were over-hit, and frustration was growing as quickly as the pace of the game was diminishing.

That is, apart from one player, who stood out like a shiny penny.

A shiny penny that paid £3.50 a week to experience the love of the game that saw him grace some of the world's greatest stadiums.

But here he was, six months after injury forced him to end a career where he shared a dressing-room with the likes of Javier Saviola, Kevin Phillips and Gareth Southgate.

Here he was showing glimpses of the cultured left-foot that made him a folk hero at Sunderland, not three miles away from this Sunday League pitch.

Here he was, pirouetting on the ball, twisting and turning, finding time and space where other players only found toil and trouble.

Here in Sunderland Sunday League's second division, shining in the colours of the Willow Pond, here was Julio Arca.

Unwittingly, the Argentinian, six months after retiring, had started on a path that would give him a silver-laden Indian Summer to his career and a long-awaited appearance at Wembley.

Arca arrived in England during the summer of 2000 and joined Sunderland for a fee of around £3.5m.

The Argentina Under-20 international was an unknown quantity to most involved in Premier League football and he took his time to settle into life in the Premier League.

He said "I got to play against the likes of David Beckham, Thierry Henry and Paul Scholes.

"Me, a young kid from Argentina, it was so exciting.

"On the pitch is the same anywhere in the world, football has its own language and it doesn't matter if you are English, Spanish or Argentinian.

"You find a way to communicate on the pitch.

"The lifestyle was complicated, getting to know the people here and the weather took me a while to get used to.

"The accent didn't matter to me, I couldn't understand anything anyway.

"I knew I had sacrifices to make by moving to a foreign country and playing the game I love at a club I didn't know too much about.

"Everybody loves football in Argentina, it is a passion and everyone always talks about it.

"I wasn't sure what to expect here, but then I found something special.

"There were 48,000 at my debut against West Ham and we were getting full crowds every two weeks.

"I got to know how big the club was, how high we were fighting in the Premier League and we knew we could compete with anyone.

"We were competing with Arsenal and Manchester United and then there was the derby against Newcastle.

"We won 2-1 at Newcastle in my first derby, when Alan Shearer missed the last-minute penalty and I quickly realised just what football meant to the region."

Arca became a cult hero on Wearside and took little time to endear himself to the Stadium of Light faithful.

He scored on his debut to put the Black Cats ahead in a 1-1 draw against West Ham United and he would go on to make over 150 appearances for the club.

Relegation from the Premier League in 2006 led to Arca's departure as he made the short switch to Middlesbrough and he would spend the next seven years of his career at the Riverside Stadium.

A foot injury brought an end to his professional career in 2013 and that was where his journey into Sunday League football began.

"I stopped playing in 2013 and I had a few months off, but without ever thinking about playing again.

"I started my coaching badges and then a friend asked me if I would play Sunday League.

"I signed the forms for the Willow Pond and then I started playing week-after-week.

"I enjoyed it, we did well and got promoted and we got a lot of attention.

"It was weird for everyone, but it took me back to playing when I was a kid.

"They were good lads and the mentality was like it was when I was younger."

The appetite for football had clearly never left Arca, nor had his desire to compete at the highest level he could.

Ebac Northern League Division Two club South Shields were looking for a statement signing.

Fresh from receiving a much-needed financial boost from local businessman

PREMIER CLASS

Geoff Thompson, the club had ambitions of rising up the non-league pyramid.

Manager Jon King and Thompson himself both had talks with Arca to persuade him to join the club.

The move came to fruition and, just as he had on his first appearance for Sunderland 14 years earlier, the midfielder made a scoring debut for the Mariners in a 1-1 draw against Stokesley Sports Club.

A new period of his career was underway.

"Jon King always tried to get me to South Shields," he explained.

"My fitness was good, I always looked after myself whether I was playing or not.

"That was the easy part, but I had to get used to training twice a week again and I knew this was another step higher in the ladder.

"I joined them and the first season was pretty good.

"I scored on my debut against Stokesley, it was an amazing season but I didn't know much about the club.

"That was the start of our journey and I knew we would get attention if we did well.

"The fans got involved, the place was starting to lift and everybody knew it."

Promotion and the Northern League Division Two title were secured within his first season at Mariners Park.

It was during that campaign that Arca had his first experience of the FA Vase, as his side bravely went out of the competition against the eventual winners Morpeth Town.

The two sides played out a titanic tie, sharing six goals over 120 minutes, before the Highwaymen came out on top with a 10-9 win in an equally epic penalty shoot-out.

It was a new experience for Arca.

"I had never heard of the FA Vase.

"I knew about non-league and Sunday League, but I didn't believe that a non-league footballer would ever play at Wembley.

"When I started playing for South Shields, and we started playing in the Vase, I couldn't believe that it was possible.

"I had never been near Wembley as a player with a club, but football can take you to places you can't ever imagine."

The Mariners would gain revenge over Morpeth during the following season as the two sides were pulled out of the hat for a fourth round tie.

NORTHERN GOAL

Controversy would follow and one of the most talked about Vase ties in recent history would be struck from the records.

With eight minutes left on the clock, Morpeth striker Liam Henderson struck to give the Highwaymen a 4-2 lead against a South Shields side that had been reduced to ten men after Arca was shown a red card.

What followed was one of the most infamous incidents in North East non-league football.

Just as Henderson's effort hit the net and his celebrations began, the floodlights went out.

The tie was abandoned, much to the chagrin of everyone connected with Morpeth Town.

The Football Association ruled that the game had to be replayed and, with Mariners Park's floodlights still undergoing maintainance, the tie was played at Morpeth's Craik Park.

The Mariners eased to a 4-0 win as two goals apiece from Gavin Cogdon and David Foley.

Arca was left in disbelief at what had gone on, but understood why the Highwaymen were left angry by the events.

"I have never experienced anything like that in football, nothing like it.

"If I was a Morpeth Town player or fan, I would have been angry.

"That's me being honest.

"They were winning, it was an equal game, but they were winning and I had been sent-off by the referee.

"They scored, the lights went off and there were a lot of discussions about what happened.

"As a player, you really want to find out, but nobody knows.

"I don't know, nobody knows, but I understand why Morpeth were so angry.

"They were so close to going through and they should have gone through, but the FA rules are the rules."

Momentum was building and a travelling band of merry Mariners made their way to the south coast for the fifth round tie against Team Solent.

Arca rounded off a 5-2 win with a 45-yard chip over the opposing goalkeeper, a goal he admits was the best of his career.

United Counties Premier League side Newport Pagnall Town were put to the sword in the quarter-final as the Mariners sent themselves through the last four with a 6-1 win at Mariners Park.

Midland League promotion challengers Coleshill Town stood between Arca and his dream of walking out at Wembley.

They did things the hard way in the first-leg in Leicestershire, coming from behind to claim a 2-1 win thanks to goals from David Foley and Andrew Stephenson.

An expectant Mariners Park awaited the second-leg a week later.

Just under 3,500 supporters packed the place out and willed their side on to a 4-0 win.

Arca got the scoring underway just before half-time with a vicious left-foot effort from the edge of the area.

Cogdon, Foley and Carl Finnigan added their names to the score-sheet, meaning a Wembley appearance was in the bag long before the full-time whistle was blown.

The celebrations got underway and Arca was left visably moved by his side's achievement.

"The first-leg was hard on an artificial pitch, but we managed to get a good result.

"But at home, we totally controlled the game.

"I got the first goal and I never really scored because I was playing deep in midfield.

"I remember it was a long ball and it got pulled back, so I thought I would go and make a run.

"The ball missed a couple of players and I closed my eyes and wished for the best.

"Luckily it went in.

"It was a massive game and the noise was phenomenal.

"I was emotional at full-time because I had got to Wembley, but it was more about the hard work people at the club had put in.

"The club could have died and I don't think people could even dream that we would get to Wembley when they were in Peterlee.

"I was thinking about them, I was thinking what it meant for them and the fans.

"It meant everything to the people that kept the club alive in Peterlee."

Cleethorpes Town would be the opposition on the Mariners historic day.

Arca had experienced all there is at the top end of the game.

He had made just under 150 appearances in the Premier League and featured in an FA Cup semi-final.

NORTHERN GOAL

He played in numerous Tyne-Wear derbies and even captained the Argentina Under-20s to a World Cup triumph in 2001.

But a first club appearance at Wembley set the nerves jangling as he looked to deliver a trophy for a staggering travelling support.

"I had nerves, my legs were like jelly at Wembley.

"I couldn't relax, I saw the stadium and I was like 'wow!'

"It is the house of English football and it wasa privilege to be there.

"We had concentrated on winning the league and other cups, but now this was Wembley.

"It was exciting for the town and we couldn't let them down.

"It was such a hot day and it was a perfect day for football and a perfect day for the fans.

"I knew we would have at least 15,000 supporters there.

"They were right in front of us as we came out of the tunnel.

"I remember playing in the FA Cup semi-final for Sunderland against Millwall and it was exactly the same.

"But it didn't happen for us and we didn't win the game.

"We had to do it for the South Shields supporters because they had given us such great support."

The Mariners looked confident as they stepped out on to the pitch.

A historic quadruple was in their sights, with their Wembley appearance coming on the back of a Northern League title win and the club lifting both the Durham Challenge Cup and the Brooks Mileson Memorial League Cup.

The big Wembley pitch suited their quick passing style and Arca was the conductor of the orchestra, spraying passes around the hallowed turf and probing for space in a packed Cleethorpes defence.

His side were in control, but it took them until two minutes before half-time to go ahead.

A foul on Cogdon saw a penalty awarded and Carl Finnigan coolly slotted the spot-kick beyond Owls keeper Liam Higton.

Despite their slender advantage, an equaliser was never really threatened and a Dillon Morse goal ended the game as a contest with ten minutes to go.

David Foley rounded off a dominant display with two goals in the last four minutes to give his side the biggest FA Vase Final win since Whitley Bay's 6-1 win over Wroxham in 2009.

"We were always in control," explained Arca

"We just needed the first goal to arrive and it did with the penalty.

"We dominated them physically in the second-half and I was feeling tired, but it was more about the tension than physical tiredness.

"The pitch is big and playing the way we played was hard work.

"But I was at Wembley, I couldn't stop running and fighting for the club and the supporters.

"We always felt comfortable and they had very few chances.

"They started going down with cramp and it's like boxing.

"When you see someone in pain and they show you that, you take advantage of that weakness.

"We knew that was our chance and the second goal told us that we had won the game.

"Dillon Morse scored the header and we knew, you could tell in the celebrations.

"We had more time on the ball, they were done as a team.

"Then Foley scored the last two and we had done it."

Four trophies, a Wembley appearance and a captain's display in the final.

It had been some season for Arca and his side, but there was one last moment of glory for the Argentinan as he got to lift the Vase.

"At full-time, it was relief.

"I just looked at the sky and thanked god that all of our hard work had paid off.

"It was a long season and I don't think anyone will ever achieve what we achieved for a long, long time.

"You used to sit, as a boy, and watch players lifting cups at Wembley, it was the stuff of dreams.

"Climbing those steps, lifting the Vase, it was a dream for me.

"Four titles, 18,000 fans at Wembley, I don't think anyone at that level will do it again."

Arca played on for another twelve months and helped South Shields to a third consecutive promotion as they secured the Evo-Stik NPL First Division North title.

He announced his retirement from the game in the summer of 2018 and brought down the curtain on a remarkable spell with the Mariners.

He left his mark on the club, just as much as they had left a mark on him.

"Playing for South Shields reminded me of how football used to be and how it should still be.

"There was a connection between the club and the fans and that helped us in every game.

"Football at a higher level isn't like that now.

"When we played at Wembley, we had thousands of fans behind us and we felt like they were with us on the pitch.

"It was very special to win the FA Vase for them because we felt like we had all achieved something together."

Not a bad tale for a Sunday league footballer.

2018

THE END?

THE END?

The sun shone brightly through Wembley's famous arch as the final whistle was blown to bring down the curtain on the 2018 FA Vase final.

Just two years earlier, as Morpeth Town were becoming the latest Northern League side to win the competition, Stockton Town were celebrating promotion from the Wearside League.

The club that had tried and failed to reach the Northern League on three separate occasions, only to be left frustrated and disappointed by strict ground-grading regulations.

A club that boasted a squad made up of players that had progressed through their own youth system.

Now here they were, at the home of English football, bidding to become the tenth different North East club to bring the Vase back to the region.

A fairy tale in the making.

But there was to be no fairy tale ending to this story.

A first-half penalty from Thatcham Town striker Shane Cooper-Clark condemned the Anchors to becoming only the fifth North East club to lose a Vase final.

They followed in the footsteps of Bedlington Terriers, Guisborough Town, Tow Law Town and West Auckland Town by leaving Wembley empty-handed.

But the full-time whistle brought a mixture of emotions for club chairman Martin Hillerby as he watched on from the royal box.

There was disappointment, but there was great pride too.

He explained "When the final whistle went, you are a bit stunned about what has happened on the day.

"We struggled to take it in, a new club like us, we hadn't experienced a final on that level.

"The defeat wouldn't define our club, we wouldn't allow it to define our club.

"There was so much that we learnt from that day and from the experience.

"The day maybe got away from us a bit, but we did ourselves justice.

"The publicity it gave the town and the club has set us in good stead for the future.

"The town has rallied behind us; the club keeps going in the right direction and we will be back.

"As I said, that defeat won't define our future."

What the future holds for the North East's love affair with the FA Vase is difficult to predict.

NORTHERN GOAL

The restructure of the non-league pyramid will see many of the Northern League clubs plying their trade at a higher-level in the near-future.

Given the strength of the league and its member clubs, it seems likely that many will follow the example of the likes of Spennymoor Town, South Shields and Morpeth Town by establishing themselves in the Evo-Stik Northern Premier League and beyond.

The storm clouds are gathering, and the sun may well be setting on the Northern League's dominance of the FA Vase.

But the stories created by the clubs that enjoyed their own day in the sun will go on for decades to come.

THE END

ACKNOWLEDGEMENTS

Writing Northern Goal has become a challenging task, but also a labour of love. However, I wouldn't have been able to do so without the support of a number of people.

Firstly, I have to thank all 12 of the former players and managers that opened up so much and for making themselves available for interviews.

Ian Crumplin, Bill Cawthra, Harry Dunn, Ian Chandler, Mark Taylor, Paul Chow, Lee Kerr, Billy Irwin, Jason Ainsley, Gareth Bainbridge, Chris Swailes and Julio Arca.

Your stories all add something unique and your achievements should be an inspiration to North East non-league players for years to come.

I'd also like to thank the photographers that provided images free of charge, meaning that both the If U Care Share Foundation and the Motor Neurone Disease Association will receive more much-needed funds.

David Nelson, Julian Tyley, Kevin Wilson, Ken Fitzpatrick, Ian Warde, Neil Thaler and Andy Nunn

There has also been valuable support from some wonderful press officers around the club, who made my job so much easier and took away a lot of the stress of putting the book together.

There was outstanding support from key figures within the Ebac Northern League.

Mike Snowdon and Gavin Perry, you have been brilliant throughout and your hard work for the league does not go unnoticed.

I also have to thank Liam Grieves for his outstanding design work from first to last. He took on the role at short notice and overhauled the look of Northern Goal to make it look so much more professional than any ideas I had.

Your work is an absolute credit to your commitment and ability as a designer.

Finally, I would like to thank my family for their unwavering support throughout the nine months it has taken to put Northern Goal together.

During that time, I became a Dad for the second time and that will always remain a special part of Northern Goal.

To my wife Jacqueline, my son William, and my baby daughter Evie, I can not thank you enough for being there for me.

Kind regards

Mark Carruthers

Printed in Great Britain
by Amazon

80067926R00076